THE **7** VIRTUES of a
PHILOSOPHER QUEEN

A woman's guide to

living & leading

in an illogical world

BARBARA STEGEMANN

Courtney!

You are a Philosopher Queen! Write me any time. Best wishes! Barb S

The 7 Virtues

Published by The 7 Virtues Communications Group
6 Carriageway Court, Bedford, Nova Scotia, B4A 3V4
Canada

www.the7virtues.com

First published in 2008

Printed in China

Library and Archives Canada Cataloguing in Publication

Stegemann, Barbara, 1969-
The 7 virtues of a philosopher queen : a woman's guide to
living & leading in an illogical world / Barbara Stegemann.

Includes bibliographical references.
ISBN 978-0-9782519-0-1

1. Leadership in women. 2. Success--Philosophy. 3. Virtues.
4. Women--Conduct of life. 5. Self-actualization (Psychology) in women. I. Title. II.
Title: Seven virtues of a philosopher queen.

HQ1221.S72 2008 305.4201 C2008-900230-X

Credits:
The publisher wishes to thank the following people for permission to print their interviews: Nasima Nastoh, Irene Barr, Diane Thorne, Lisa Palleson-Stallan, Jovilyn Mercy Culasing, Debbie Lepore and Dr. Colin Starnes.
The publisher wishes to thank the YWCA Halifax, UNSM, The Nova Scotia Advisory Council on the Status of Women, and Service Nova Scotia and Municipal Relations for the use of the report "Untapped Resources; Women and Municipal Government in Nova Scotia."

Typeset by: Reuben Hall Design, Halifax, Nova Scotia
Cover Design by: Karyon Group, Vancouver, British Columbia
Edited by: Peggy MacKinnon, Halifax, Nova Scotia

Barb Stegemann should be running Canada. It's no coincidence that 7 Virtues launches March 8th. Just happens to be International Women's Day and women is what Barb is all about. Actually she's about women and power, the loss of it and the regaining of personal and professional power. Years from now, if social thinkers are speaking and writing about a change in the power profile of women, you need look no further than The 7 Virtues of a Philosopher Queen *for starting the ball rolling. It does beg the question, how the hell can a woman so busy find the time to write a book so complex and funny? What kind of person has the time to change the world AND outwork all those around her? Ladies (and gentlemen) I give you Barb Stegemann, Philosopher Queen.*

– TERRY DAVID MULLIGAN, Canadian Broadcaster, Vancouver

Barb Stegemann motivates and inspires women (and men) of all ages and backgrounds. She lives her philosophy in thought, word and deed. Her passionate treatise will shake you up and provide you with practical steps to ignite positive action in your life, family, workplace and community.

– PROFESSOR KIM KIERANS, Director, University of King's College School of Journalism, Halifax

We had Barb Stegemann in for the last half hour of the show and wow, what a dynamic person!! It was great to listen to her and she was so fresh and was a straight talker, I really enjoyed it. She was nice too, which is always a bonus! Here is the link to her new book coming out next March and if you click on "Meet the author" you will find her e-mail address in order to help her on her crusade to cure the world of the cancer that is bullying. Good luck, Barb!

– AMBER LEBLANC'S BLOG, The Rick Howe Show, Halifax

Passionately positive and intensely engaging, Barb Stegemann is a motivational tour de force. Since her return to Atlantic Canada fresh from numerous economic and social development triumphs in British Columbia, I have been fascinated by the way she has entranced, enthralled and encouraged her fellow citizens to rediscover their inner spark and embark on a quest for excellence. This book is much like Barb herself—it serves as a powerful touchstone that gently yet irrevocably forces you to look inward. And with that introspection, comes an unavoidable awareness that each of us is a potential agent of change. For groups and for individuals, this book delivers—in plainspoken language and commonsense wisdom—philosophical direction that can change your life. Follow Barb's direction, live the 7 virtues and you'll learn to embrace the leader within!

– DAWN CHAFE, EDITOR, *Atlantic Business Magazine*, St. John's

Named by BC Business Magazine as one of the province's life shifters, Barb Stegemann would put the reinvention of matriarch Madonna to shame. Local businesswoman, motivational speaker, columnist, and author of The 7 Virtues of a Philosopher Queen: A woman's guide to living & leading in an illogical world, *Barb is a multi-achiever whose positive outlook, inspired by stoic philosopher Marcus Aurelius, is simple: Everyone and everything is brought to you for a reason. Either to teach you or to bear.*

– MARY-JO DIONNE, Editor *The Block Magazine*, Vancouver

Readers looking for a path to a brighter future for themselves and their community will find The 7 Virtues of a Philosopher Queen *a compass on which they can depend.*

– STEVE PROCTOR, Business Editor, *The Chronicle Herald*, Halifax

PHILOSOPHER QUEEN

❋

A woman who is rational under any circumstances

❋

She uses reason over emotion

❋

She is grounded in self-awareness and authenticity

❋

This enables her to lead through challenges and transition

❋

Her self-awareness allows her to assess and
take on risks and challenges

❋

Her philosophical direction is the crucial
foundation for living *The Good Life*

TABLE OF CONTENTS

DEDICATION

This book is dedicated to Captain Trevor Greene, my long time mentor, friend and inspiration. Captain Greene risked his life to liberate women in Afghanistan from the most extreme version of patriarchal society—terrorism.

While sitting in a peaceful Shura with the village elders, discussing how to bring clean drinking water, education and health care to the women and children of the village, Trevor was attacked from behind. A man who did not want the people of his community to have free thought or free will struck him in the head with a Taliban axe.

Now as my best friend works daily to relearn how to walk, his friends are keeping his dream alive that no one—no man, woman, or child, is oppressed or bullied by anyone.

Trevor, your voice is being heard. Your mission was not in vain. The daily small successes will add up to the big Victory. You have inspired us all to see what matters and for that we are so very grateful to you and for your work.

INTRODUCTION

In the upcoming prologue of this book, Barb Stegemann comes right out and says it: "If asked if I am a feminist, I say no." That line floored me.

How can someone like Barb—someone who escaped childhood poverty, overcame obesity, launched her own successful business, spearheaded a national anti-bullying campaign *and* founded Citizens for Halifax, the first non-partisan civic society in the history of Nova Scotia (and that's just a few of her accomplishments)—how can she *not* be a feminist?

I am a feminist. I believe in equal pay for work of equal value, and I believe oppression against women still exists in today's world—oppression that must be overcome through activism and advocacy. But here's the thing: *The 7 Virtues of a Philosopher Queen* supports both our views.

Barb isn't against the emancipation of women—far from it. What she rejects are the distortions that feminism has imposed on the relationship between men and women. And she believes that women can learn valuable lessons from men by embracing the time-honoured philosophies that shape today's worlds of business and government—where most of the major decisions that impact women are made.

Barb Stegemann is living proof of the power of the *7 Virtues* to help every woman set and achieve any goal, big or small. By embracing the virtues of **Wonder, Moderation, Truth, Courage, Justice, Wisdom** and **Beauty,** she has overcome adversity, found love, and established herself as a professional force to be reckoned with. She has done this through the guidance of men who have mentored and coached her throughout that incredible journey.

This book is about the emancipation of women—and that starts with you. Whoever you are, and wherever you are in your life, *The 7 Virtues of a Philosopher Queen* will guide you through a process of self-discovery that will give you the tools to shape your own future—personally, professionally and spiritually.

> – PEGGY MACKINNON, Professional Writer,
> Publicist & Philosopher Queen

On becoming a Philosopher Queen

We have all encountered those special people who display the character needed to get through hardships and life's challenges. In fact, these people not only endure, they seem to rise and soar over the hurdles in front of them. Regardless of their culture, socio-economic level or gender, these people possess the character needed to advance their lives and ultimately the lives of those around them.

If you ask yourself what it is about these people who demonstrate leadership and can navigate through obstacles with grace and dignity, you will find they live with philosophical direction—they live *The 7 Virtues.*

Wonder

Moderation

Truth

Courage

Justice

Wisdom

Beauty

Just as in a proven scientific formula, the virtues share universal properties that can be captured and lived by each and every one of us no matter our position in life. If lived out, the virtues guarantee you will achieve levels of living and greatness you may have only glimpsed before.

This book is a move towards inspiring women to become personally and professionally empowered so we may then enhance the lives of the people we care about. Women are the nucleus of the family. When we want to reach children, husbands, teenagers and aging parents, we communicate through women and mothers. And somewhere in there, after they've taken up the interests of those around them, women take care of themselves. *The 7 Virtues of a Philosopher Queen* reverses that equation by proposing a model that first nurtures the nucleus—the female centre of the family. Empowered to take care of the people around them, women are able to build a foundation of support. With the foundation firmly in place, women, in turn, may then go out and take on positions of leadership in the community, government and business and lead with success. That is what this book is about.

There is no lack of desire for women to lead; we just need to learn the language of entry into the networks of business and government and ultimately to shape that language to ensure that women overcome barriers.

In the following chapters on the virtues you will discover how you can advance yourself personally and professionally through the philosophical virtues. You will also see how your own personal and professional advancement fits into the bigger picture of advancing society. For the philosophers see the interests of the individual as one with the interests of society. Philosophers understand that we advance ourselves most when we concurrently recognize our roles in advancing the world around us. Through *The 7 Virtues of a Philosopher Queen* you will gain insights through real life stories and through exercises that you can apply to advance yourself and the society in which you live.

> *For a life that is sound and secure, cultivate a thorough insight into things and discover their essence, matter and cause; put your whole heart into doing what is just, and speaking what is true; and for the rest know the joy of life by piling good deed on good deed until no rift or cranny appears between them.*

– MARCUS AURELIUS

Philosophy for women

*Employ your time in improving yourself by other men's writing so
that you shall come easily by what others have laboured hard for.*

– SOCRATES

Both Socrates and Plato believed that philosophy is the key to happiness and the welfare of humans. Socrates stood by the belief that
philosophy makes people more virtuous and happier than anything
else. In fact, he was willing to die for his beliefs rather than compromise his ethics.

When I studied philosophy in University, I was taught by eccentric,
stodgy male professors who loomed over us at our Cambridge-style
University of King's College in Halifax, Nova Scotia. They wore *Harry
Potteresque* gowns and looked upwards while using a nasal undertone
and eccentric animation as they reflected and pontificated. Being of
humble roots from rural Nova Scotia, I found all this ceremony and
tradition to be a refreshing new way of looking at the world. It wasn't
better or worse—it was just different.

The life of the mind was such a departure from my childhood focus
on trying to exist in poverty. This focus on the quest for the meaning
of our existence seemed to be so playful. Imagine delighting in the
intellect rather than the basic animal needs of a human to survive. Yet
something was amiss. I could not explain it at the time. As much as I
loved all the stodgy intellectualism, I noticed that the women in the
class, although smart, still felt somewhat foreign in this male world of
philosophy. Perhaps it had something to do with the fact that not one
of the philosophers on the extensive reading list was a woman. Yet,
there had been great female philosophers, albeit few, and their works
were out there. Still, I managed to glean much and adapt to it.

If you really break down philosophy and the strength of the philosophical mind, it is about putting body and soul and intellect into a
relationship whereby the intellect informs the body and soul. This
idea provided me with the fullest understanding of why I embraced

philosophy. I was moving away from a life that focused upon daily physical needs and began embracing the philosophical concept of the mind/soul and the focus on building strength of character. I was moving away from a focus on "existence" towards the "meaning" of existence. It costs nothing to build up your character. This is why there is so much potential for philosophy to be incorporated into our everyday lives. And this is why philosophy is for everyone, regardless of our socio-economic status or gender.

If philosophy can lift us out of the cares of daily physical poverty, as in Plato's cave analogy (Chapter I), then it can most certainly lift us out of focusing our energies on body image and the superficial collecting of things.

As with other women studying philosophy back in my university days, I was already drawn to more of a male kind of thinking. Perhaps this can be attributed to adversity as a child as well as my Generation X upbringing. So I lived out the next 17 years believing that I was no different than men and could do anything I put my mind to.

Then it happened.

I was introduced to my first women's group.

I attended the Women's Political Campaign School in Vancouver, British Columbia. While defending my position on how women are no different than men, a seasoned politician reminded me that she and many women before me had broken down the walls for us younger women to pass through. It dawned on me for the first time that I could not enjoy my liberties unless the women ahead of me had blazed the trails for us to finally enter into the worlds of business and government.

I began to watch these women as they worked towards equal representation in government in order to ensure that the needs of women and children were met. I started to see how this very group who had broken down barriers for Generation X women like me was beginning to lose its ground.

My generation of women, many of whom see themselves as no different than males, see groups of women working towards equality as a contradiction in terms. In our ideal world, women and men can work together with a shared goal of equal representation, not equality.

Once I began to realize that men and women working together was the answer, I started to see that the politician at the campaign school was right. Some men of the older generation, as well as those who preserve that cultural way of thinking, continue to build the walls. I was left wondering whether the walls were intended to keep women out or not. Would the pioneer women politicians look at today and think that their chapter is done and that to move forward, women must scale the walls with men? And then I realized, the only way to ultimately overcome these obstacles would be through partnership with men.

Partnerships developed through an understanding of the philosophical thinking that has shaped the current patriarchal thinking will be our first step. Our mothers did not sit down with us as young girls and discuss Adam Smith and capitalism or Plato and the polis (politics). Therefore, it is up to us to learn this language and to shape it.

On feminism

I'd like to address a question that may be running through your mind—is this a book on feminism? The answer is no.

If asked if I am a feminist, I say no. I find that most women and men don't even really understand the word. The word scares many men—the very men we're trying both to learn from and to enlighten. Some of history's most incredible philosophers such as Mary Wollstonecraft and Simone de Beauvoir were labeled feminists and excluded from the reading lists of philosophy courses. Instead they were listed under feminism and women's studies, thus isolating their books from those very men who need to be reading these great works.

We must not forget the courageous women who opened the doors for us. I am grateful to know so many wonderful women who do consider themselves feminists and who have helped us get to this point. Now it is important for us to become enlightened. As enlightened people, we see that men are not the problem. The problems are the learned cultural habits that we allow to live on such as sexism and a patriarchal society. All of us have a role in shifting from living the myth, for it is *both* men and women who contribute to the patriarchal society. What it will take are men who will, in partnership with women, work to reach the objective of equal representation. And it will take enlightened men and women to make a shift out of this patriarchy to a more egalitarian culture.

Our task, as women, is to summon up the courage to be accountable and take responsibility for advancing the thinking of those around us. When we enlighten rather than condemn, we will accelerate ourselves to a place of equal representation in society. Through this equal representation and a shared political will, we will narrow the gap between rich and poor—which is often the root of war and oppression.

If any feminist is reading this and growing uncomfortable, I ask you to merely understand that I want the great teachings of male and female philosophers to be accessible and accepted by all. That starts with dropping the labels of the past and ensuring the message is delivered in a more accessible way for both men and women.

I would like to add that if it were not for the amazing male professors who inspired me 20 years ago in university, I could not have put this book together. You will see interviews and comments from professors from my former university. I applaud them, for they list female philosophers in their current curricula and have created philosophy programs such as Humanities 101 for people living in poverty who would never otherwise have had the opportunity to be exposed to this kind of empowering philosophical thinking.

Why a book on philosophy for women? The answer is that there is no modern book on philosophy with the sole purpose of empowering everyday women with the foundations of philosophy that they can apply to their current challenges. Most philosophy books make reference to men and the qualities and characteristics men have but do not examine the concerns women face about our children, parents, and partners. With the belief that philosophy is the foundation to self-discovery, then it would stand to reason that women seeking a life of meaning should have a woman's book on philosophy with the goal of empowering women to work in partnership with men to advance society. Men have had hundreds and hundreds of years of access to male-oriented philosophy. It is now women's turn to have access to the teachings that have shaped our current worlds of business and government and make it their own. The purpose is to ensure every-day women are also provided with the opportunity to live with philo-sophical direction. Men are also encouraged to read *The 7 Virtues of a Philosopher Queen* for not all men have had the opportunity to learn about the teachings of great male and female philosophers.

There is a language that is spoken in the patriarchal society in busi-ness and politics. It is a language rooted in philosophical thinking and in order for women to move forward in this current patriarchal system, it's crucial to learn the language. This will also empower us to help make a smoother shift to equal representation with men in society.

The following two quotations reflect cultures separated by more than two centuries. Yet, they both echo the same sentiment: that as women, we need to place a higher value on our ideas, on leadership, reason and intellect over material things in order to take our rightful place in society.

> *It is time to effect a revolution in female manners -*
> *Time to restore them to their lost dignity -*
> *and make them,*
> *As a part of the human species*

– MARY WOLLSTONECRAFT, 1792

> *What happened to the dream of a girl president?*
> *She's dancing in the video next to 50 cent*
> *They travel in packs of two or three*
> *With their itsy bitsy doggies and their teeny weenie tees*
> *Where oh where have the smart people gone?"*

– PINK, Song–Stupid Girls, 2006

The quotation from the 18th Century philosopher, Mary Wollstone-craft, shows us how the strides we have taken as women in society will become significant when we fully participate in a revolution of female manners.

The issues that Wollstonecraft brought to the forefront of her book, *A Vindication of the Rights of Woman*, reveal that, over two centuries after her day, some of our own issues still exist. When listening to the song "Stupid Girls," by pop-idol Pink, it echoes the same message of Wollstonecraft that we, women, are still facing the sometimes self-imposed challenges of centuries past and not advancing ourselves. This we will examine further in the chapters on **Moderation** and **Beauty**.

When we put too much energy on the physical and not the intellectual or soul, we waste precious energy and miss out on so many gratifying opportunities and a life full of joy with purpose and meaning.

I am very grateful to have had some of the most incredible mentors in my life, both male and female. It was through my observations of these wise women and men that I began to notice the virtues they lived by and was profoundly moved by how the practice of these virtues had led them to success and happiness.

The 7 Virtues–Wonder, Moderation, Truth, Courage, Justice, Wisdom and Beauty, if practiced, will take you to the most wonderful experiences.

We will begin with **Wonder,** as it's crucial to wonder rather than doubt. Then **Moderation** as this is the key to balance and keeping everything from money matters to weight in check. Then on to **Truth,** as this is what we should set out to seek at all times. Once you know the truth, it will most certainly take **Courage** to communicate it. The reward of communicating courage is **Justice**. Once you have ensured justice has prevailed, you receive the gift of **Wisdom**. This being a book for women, we know **Beauty** is something many of us grapple with. I wanted to take a philosophical look at beauty in the way Michelangelo would look at a work of art, beautiful in and of itself, with mind, body and soul in harmony.

Here is where we begin to realize the importance of our own accountability in our actions as women. I cannot overstate the importance of observing successful men and women who lead lives of character and using their example to incorporate all that's good about men and women in the advancement of women in shaping a just society.

Women have far to go to attain equal representation in business and in government. The root of the advancement of women will be found in the foundations of philosophical direction. In other words, personal accountability for our gender, and of course, the wise observation of what has worked for men in business and government will be important factors in reaching equal representation.

The 7 Virtues of a Philosopher Queen is not to go in-depth as an academic research paper would on the differences between men and women. Instead, this is intended as a realistic and usable guide for women to navigate their advancement in business and government and in other areas, from education to the non-profit sector.

I want to take a fresh approach to how we can truly advance women and the people we care about by emulating what successful men and women do in their lifetime practice of leadership. For the virtues take daily practice. Wise leaders hone the virtues every day and see every challenge to the virtues as an opportunity to strengthen them. It requires daily practice no matter what the challenge.

Your network is your net worth

Expanding your network to include men in leadership roles can directly increase your net worth. You will learn of the importance of women establishing relations and partnerships with males on their own playing field to build up peer-to-peer respect.

Communicating within the long-established male-dominated worlds of business and government will not only advance you personally, but it will advance the organizations you serve. Men have been and continue to be the dominant force in the business world, government and even media at the upper management levels. Women have certainly made great strides through persistence and knowledge, but have yet to achieve equal representation in media, government, business or positions of power.

We can learn a great deal by observing the solid networks men create. Women who can integrate these principles will increase the reach of their own networks. A close look at the philosopher, Jean-Jacques Rousseau's "The Social Contract" in the chapter on **Justice** will show how we, as women, can connect with these types of networks to narrow the gap between rich and poor.

Your network will most certainly affect your net worth and the health and wealth of the organization you represent.

Today's Visionary Change Agents are those women and men who see the Gender Power Shift coming. They will be the ones who will capitalize upon this to advance both themselves and society. They will be the champions of a healthy society where they rise to the top of their game and consistently enhance the lives of the people around them along the way.

Building a philosophical foundation

L ong before today's patriarchal male structure of western civilization evolved, *women* ruled! As today's modern-day scholars predict
the shifting away from a patriarchal society, women of philosophical
direction are positioned to become leaders in a more egalitarian society. These women will be important in shaping the transition to the
new society through the establishment of networks that will benefit
both men and women. Solid networks that bridge the gap between
rich and poor will be built by women of character who incorporate
The 7 Virtues into their lives personally and professionally.

The 7 Virtues of a Philosopher Queen maps out how women in today's
Western Society can foster and develop the qualities and character
needed to make positive changes in both their personal and professional lives that will lead ultimately to the advancement of society.

These women will have to be special human beings indeed.

The ancient philosophers have shown us that one of the most evident
signs of a leader is an inclination toward philosophical thinking. It is
the philosopher above all others who is able to ask the right questions
about human life and can therefore make judgements on what is true
and best in *any* given situation.

A Philosopher Queen is a person who is grounded in self-awareness
and authenticity. This enables her to lead through challenges and
transition. Because leaders need to be self-aware to assess and take
on risk and challenges, philosophy is a crucial foundation for great
living and successful leadership.

Philosophy allows us to let go of any preconceived beliefs or judgements of what is right or wrong and make sound decisions based on
each unique challenge we face. The ultimate reward of becoming a
philosopher is living *the good life*.

Your character is your destiny

Philosophers believe that change is absoluteley imperative to growth.

Leaders who can accept and adapt to change are the ones who can readily move themselves and their communities or projects forward in times of transition. Organizations are often likened to individuals. They are as healthy as the individuals who lead them and as strong as the foundations they are built upon. As individuals, we stretch and grow and adapt to change or we are doomed to live in the past, unable to advance. The same is true of the organizations we lead. The organization to which you belong, whether it be your family, a city, community group, educational institute or corporation, is no different than an individual in experiencing the changes that lead to growth.

We've all asked ourselves, "What is my purpose here?" Regardless of our individual scenarios, we all seek the meaning of our existence. Those with a solid sense of purpose and sense of self are the ones who meet success in their lives. Through philosophical questioning we can come to our own personal meaning and uncover our purpose.

Examined philosophical teachings on the virtues have empowered men for centuries to advance their personal and professional lives. Authored by a primarily male culture, these teachings were not as accessible to everyday women as they were available to the elite, male-dominated classes throughout time. Female philosophers were often dismissed as feminist writers, their texts listed under women's studies courses in universities rather than straight philosophy, worthy of being read by all students, male and female.

Learning the language

It is important for women to learn about the philosophical teachings of male philosophers in order to learn the "language" that has historically been the entrance point for men into business and government. That is not to say there are no great female philosophers. In fact, much of what you will find in this book links back to Mary Wollstonecraft. An 18th Century philosopher considered by many to be the mother of feminism, Wollstonecraft should have been acknowledged as a revolutionary *thinker* instead and taken her rightful place with the great male philosophers. Her message, when broken down, is based clearly upon extending the great teachings of male philosophy to women so that men and women can work together. Somewhere along the way we lost her message. It is important for today's women to reclaim this important work published ahead of its time in conjunction with the lessons from the great male philosophers to advance women in leadership roles.

Feminism champions the rights of women. It is time for all of us to champion the rights of women and men, recognizing that one of the best ways to reach everyone—men, children, aging parents and youth—is often through the nucleus of the family: the woman.

Why humans are unique—language & reason

Plato explained that we have a tripartite soul. In our three-part composition, we, as humans, are distinguished from all other beings by our capacity to use language and our ability to reason. This is our essence—this is the thing that makes humans so unique.

It would stand to reason then, that we would hone these gifts which we have been provided with, above all other species, to their fullest potential. This requires that we do not let our bodily appetites take over our ability to reason and to use language, as these are the two top-level qualities we have.

Bodily appetites such as materialism, greed, jealousy, lust, and pride can stand in the way of our own capacity for greatness. Throughout the exercises in this book, we will focus upon working on the elements of language and reason over bodily appetites to lead the good life.

Voices of authority

For those women who have *broken through* and are in positions of leadership in business, government, and the media, we often hear of the struggle to create a distinctive "voice of authority." This term is used widely by women interviewed in media articles about the process of becoming their authentic selves in leadership positions. They reveal that there are fears shared by many women that if women come across as too strong they may be perceived in a negative light. Re-examining this anxiety through a philosophical lens will enable women to stop fearing what others think and focus on building a more effective path to leadership by letting their authentic self speak.

Philosophical direction is the root to becoming our authentic selves

Strong female leadership is not at all about trying to adopt a male voice of authority. Nor is it about caring whether someone likes or dislikes you. The Philosopher Queen does not concern herself with such matters but instead moves forward with right action as opposed to trying to win friends. You are guaranteed to attract true friends if you are your authentic self so do not worry about whether someone likes you or not.

It is philosophical thinking that will empower us to become our authentic selves—something all people want and deserve. People seek leaders with a sense of direction and purpose. By taking a page from the philosophical teachings led by males throughout time, we can incorporate the kind of thinking that guides leaders regardless of gender. So it really isn't about mimicking men, but rather, examining the teachings and culture that have guided men throughout the centuries that created the current *language* of business and government. It is crucial that we learn that language by understanding the philosophical teachings that underly it. Once we understand the language we can add our own vocabulary and shape it. That is how we will meet success in business and government, in harmony with men. And having a seat at the table where the decisions are made that affect our lives will accelerate the causes that concern us rather that remaining on the fringes looking in.

When it comes to understanding the history of male success we must look deeper and see that it's really about understanding its foundation: the age-old language of business and government. The language used by men for centuries has its roots in philosophical teaching. Whether they were applying Adam Smith's theories on Capitalism, Plato's take on the polis (politics), Sun Tzu's logic on leadership in *The Art of War* or Michelangelo's perspective on art or beauty, the language used by leaders throughout the ages has been shaped by male philosophy.

Now that women are taking on more leadership roles, it is important that we learn this historic language and add our own words to shape the vocabulary for both men and women so that we can understand each other better. Since the language is rooted in philosophical thinking, there is room for women to learn its roots and to ultimately help it evolve to include women's voices in an authentic way. It is equally important for us to connect with the great female philsophers of the past and ensure that they take their rightful place in the league with the great ancient male philosophers.

On learning the language

You would not go to Spain without learning some Spanish first. But if you did go, would you be surprised if everyone spoke Spanish to you? Would you be upset and wonder why everyone wasn't speaking your language? No, you would not. Would you then walk into the world of business or government that has been historically dominated by men and wonder why they are not speaking your language?

No, you would not–or at least should not. You would learn their language as you would in any foreign land, and ultimately over time, you will not only communicate effectively, but you might just add your own new words to the vocabulary.

When I waitressed to put myself through university in the late '80s, I worked in Chinese restaurants in Halifax, Nova Scotia. I experienced the incredible work ethic of my Chinese employers and their love of a good joke, as well as the importance of working with family and including children in what the family does. They also literally taught me their language. This was crucial to my success in the restaurant. I share this story with you because it parallels the worlds of business and government in terms of learning the working language.

While at the restaurant, I had noticed that the other Chinese waitresses got all of the dim sum shifts on the weekends. These shifts were busy and they made a lot of money in tips. I wanted to make the big tip money to put myself through school, but there was only one problem–I did not speak Cantonese, the language used in these restaurants.

One very slow evening during my shift, I asked my friend, Toni (Don Lay) to teach me how to order dim sum in her language in the kitchen. She was so wonderful. In one evening she wrote out how to count to ten, and how to say everything from shrimp dumplings to chicken feet in Cantonese. I got my first dim sum shift and when I ran into the kitchen and hollered out, "Two orders of chicken feet" in Cantonese, the cooks looked at me like *I* was speaking a foreign language because they had not expected me, this over 5 foot 9 inch Amazon North American to order in Cantonese. So I repeated my order and added "Fai dee lah!!!" That means "Hurry up" in Cantonese. They burst out laughing as it was so funny! I laughed too—all the way to the bank, as I got to keep the dim sum shifts and made a lot of money to pay for my university philosophy books.

It was interesting that other North American women also wanted these shifts at the restaurant and they were told by the boss, "Go ahead, learn the language and you can reap the rewards." They never did learn the language. I want women to learn the language of business and government so that we can ensure there are more women in leadership roles.

Proposed dilema—How to avoid being called "something that rhymes with witch"

Barbara Bush once coined that famous phrase. It is amazing to hear women say that if they did what a man did, they would be alienated or hated or called every unpleasantry in the book.

Now is that really true?

Maybe. But even if it is true, the only thing we can change is the way in which we respond to outside attitudes. Philosophers Marcus Aurelius and Mary Wollstonecraft taught that you must expect to be greeted each day with interference, ingratitude, insolence, disloyalty, ill-will and selfishness. Some men go to work and are called every unpleasantry in the book. But most men regard this as a philosopher might. They pay no attention and move forward with their goals. The Philosophers would want you to remember that each person is brought to you either for you to teach or to bear. Everyone is brought into your life for a reason. One only needs to remain rational and figure out why the person was brought to you—to teach or to bear. I believe you can add "learn from" as well. And if you can remain rational about it you will better put your energies to use on positive actions so that the negative energy does not tap out the energy you have for good deeds.

If someone were to call you names and you then spent the rest of your day worrying about it or worse—talking about it—then all of the energy you needed to do your good work would be given away.

You can learn far more from someone you dislike than from someone you like. This may sound odd at first. But if someone enters your life who upsets you, step back and with no emotion or judgement, try to figure out what their message truly is.

When someone is brought into your life, they were brought in for a reason. The main way to ensure that you teach, learn from or bear this person is to remove all emotion from the situation and ask what the real message or learning is.

A Philosopher Queen is rational under any circumstance

Do not give less-than-savoury actions by others any credence. If someone says something unkind about you, do not talk of it—otherwise their action lives on. If someone says something about or to you that you find unkind, how does it actually have any bearing on who you are? Marcus Aurelius asks, "Is an emerald beautiful because we say it is beautiful?" No, it simply *is* beautiful. What we say about it, be it positive or negative, has no actual bearing on its qualities.

An emerald gem becomes no less beautiful nor more beautiful if I say it is. What I say about an emerald has no bearing on its true beauty.

Therefore, if a comment has no bearing on your life and your qualities and what has been said is not true, then why would you give it your energy and breathe life into it by talking of it? However, if the action does have a bearing on your life, do not talk of it but do reflect on what your proper course of action should be.

Lay no blame, be accountable and figure out why a person was brought into your life who may have said things of you. Reflect in order to decide what, if anything, needs to be done about it. If, upon reflection, you find that something does need to be done, then take appropriate action. You must trust that you have the right answers inside yourself to take the right course of action.

Most importantly, invest no energy in worrying. Simply move forward with your mission. And invest no energy in continuing to talk of their untrue words otherwise you are breathing life into their words. And then it becomes perceived as truth.

This is philosophy in action

The Philosopher Queen invests no energy in concerning herself with what others think of her. She simply moves forward with the work at hand. From that she earns the respect of everyone around her. She has no concern about the status quo, nor does she care about keeping up with the Joneses. She has a strong grasp of her own mission and purpose in her work and life so that she has a strong sense of self and can draw on the right answers from within. She is unwavering in her belief and trusts that she can meet success.

So instead of dropping your goals and focusing upon making everyone else happy (as we so often do), choose instead to stay the course with your goal, your mission, and know and trust that everyone will hear your authentic voice ultimately. By doing this, you will earn others' approval and support based on your own authentic motives rather than just wanting to keep everyone happy. When people back you simply because it is the right thing to do it is a much more satisfying sense of accomplishment.

Herein lies the philosophical secret

As long as your work has the greater good as an end goal and you have done your best work you can be assured that you will meet success and will have the support you seek from the people you need. Never allow anyone to compromise what you know to be right action. Stay true to what you believe your expertise, knowledge and ethics tell you to do. Stick up for what you believe is the right thing to do. And if others are not understanding this, then look at new ways to explain it—remember, it is all in the language. Never compromise what you know to be the right course of action because someone won't let you. What they are really saying is, "I don't understand, please explain it to me." So you must find new ways to explain it in their language.

I recall when I was producing for a television show I was asked to write a corporate video for a big-name company that had just produced a state-of-the-art laptop computer. I was told I had carte blanche and could write the communications piece as I saw fit. I chose to write for the consumer who wanted longevity in a product—a computer that would last for years rather than having to be updated every six months. And this product I was featuring would certainly deliver on that.

The show's sales manager then decided that I had to change the video script and write for the dot-com millionaire who wanted the newest, fastest gadgets to satisfy his/her fast-paced life. I warned him that I saw the tech bubble about to burst, but no one had labeled or declared it yet so no one believed that it could happen. Meanwhile, the dot-com millionaires were losing their shirts. I told my manager they were not a good target audience for the product. No one would listen to me; the manager chose to go with the statistics and information from six months earlier which had already become outdated. I felt that if I went along with their strategy, I would be misleading the client so I gave my two-weeks notice and went home and prepared to start a company that would help businesses adapt to their true environments. I enrolled at a local college in a program that would guide me in this new territory and did all the learning I needed to feel confident in running my own company.

I named my company Acclimatize Communications Corp. I went on to earn three times the money I was making with the TV show. I firmly believe this is a result of staying true to my ethics which are based upon the virtues outlined in the following pages. I was not going to mislead the client from my previous job and chose to stand by what I believed in even if it meant leaving my so-called "secure job." Two weeks after I left the TV show, many of the staff were laid off.

Right action—the foundation to successful living

Interestingly, everyone around me at the time I gave my notice wondered how I could leave a seemingly "secure job" and go into the unknown. I just didn't see it the same way as they did. Now this is an important point. What the world "sees" is not necessarily what is right action, and you will need to distinguish between the two as this will ultimately impact your own success and the organizations you represent. From a philosophical perspective, I was placed in a position that was going to compromise my ethics by not allowing me to show my client their true challenges and opportunities ahead. As it turned out, what appeared to be risky by leaving my job was actually the safest route. My peers were all given pink slips two weeks after I'd gone on to start my own company. They were left with no options. I was left with control over what I was doing. I was trusting my inner voice and my character which told me I could not go along with anything that compromised my work ethic.

Accountable action–key to success

By choosing not to compromise my ethics, by choosing not to mislead clients, I was led to a far better life. The most interesting piece of this is that not only did I leave that show, but I set out to do what I felt they were *not* doing, and I continued with my mission to help businesses truly adapt to challenging scenarios and change.

So it takes more than just walking away from a situation where you feel you are being asked to compromise your ethics and what you believe to be right action. It takes following your ethics in leaving, and then following through on creating a scenario for yourself where you can actualize what you believe in. I was not going to wait for someone to create a dream situation where I could help businesses truly adapt. I created it myself. I created my company!

Since 2001, I have been able to advise large corporations, non-profit and government organizations on taking proper action in strategy, communications and economic development. Past clients include Lululemon Athletica, The City of Vancouver and MITACS, the largest Networks of Centres of Excellence (NCE) in Canada.

In my work I get to think critically, independently and reflectively to ensure I lead my clients in the right direction. I did not have that luxury while working for someone else with other goals not compatible with mine. And regardless of where my career path takes me, this skill is now embedded in me. My measure is not the company or its location. My measure is ensuring I consistently surround myself with people and situations that allow me to think freely and do what I do best.

In fact, in 2007 I moved across the country and left the province of British Columbia to return to Nova Scotia to help the economy of my home province. And again, I was asked by friends and peers in BC, "How can you leave Lotusland?"

The decision took many months. Putting my company to "bed" and taking on a job with a crown corporation in Nova Scotia meant a lot of changes. And yet, what seemed on the outside to others to be a strange decision, is again another example of my choosing to follow my intuition and to stay on track with my goals.

After running my company for six years, I began to seek mentorship again. I needed to take my learning to another level and I just did not see where that was going to come from in my life in BC. I had many people who inspired me, but I did not have daily mentorship and I was ready for that. I had also made a commitment to myself as a young girl decades ago that I would one day help the economy of Nova Scotia. And I am committed to that self-promise. The image of my younger self living in poverty in rural Nova Scotia is forever etched in my work and in all that I do. If I can take my experience and connect others who face similar obstacles with ways of living to advance themselves, then I know that I am living my life's plan. Every day I see in my mind those young children living in poverty in rural Nova Scotia and for them, I do my work. That powerful visual in my mind's eye has steered me in the right direction.

It also directed me back into the path of the most ethical person I had ever met in my life–John MacDonell. At the age of 15, I met the smartest, most ethical boy I had ever come across in high school. In fact, years later I followed John to university and we had remained friends for 23 years. It was Socrates who said, "follow the smart people."

Through the tragic attack on our best friend, Captain Trevor Greene, that smart boy from all those years ago re-entered my life. And this time I thought I am not going to wait until I am 80 to tell him how I feel. So I did. Now that friend of 23 years is my partner and we live in Nova Scotia. John is a mentor to our children, a coach to me and I know first hand that you don't have to settle in life, that you can have the most glorious life if you seek out the virtues in your work life, in the people you surround yourself with and your partner. Like attracts like, so the more you work on the virtues, the more you will attract high calibre people who are stretching themselves to find the divine and good in themselves and in you.

As well, the career door opened once I made the decision to return home to Nova Scotia to be with my partner and to have mentorship.

I was offered the position of Communications Manager for Trade Centre Limited, a crown corporation that is an economic engine of the province. The CEO, Fred MacGillivray, a visionary who led the bid for the 2014 Commonwealth Games, was the mentor I was seeking and within my second day on the job, I saw a level of leadership and commitment you only read about.

On March 8, 2007, the Mayor of the day pulled out of a bid that would have won a significant catalyst for economic growth for the province— the 2014 Commonwealth Games was to bring hundreds of millions of dollars to our "have-not" province in investment and economic spinoffs. That day, my CEO had also made a previous commitment to raise funds for the Nova Scotia Paraplegic Society by taking pledges and remaining in a wheelchair all day. When my CEO received the news that the Mayor had pulled the plug on the excellent work he had done for a year and a half, he remained in the wheelchair. He made a commitment and was going to see it through. My CEO raised $30,000 dollars that day with his friends by remaining committed to a goal. The Mayor at that time cost us hundreds of millions of dollars that day due to his lack of commitment and fear.

That night at the dinner for the Nova Scotia Paraplegic Society, I sat beside my CEO and looked at him and said, "you have sealed my loyalty to this province." I gained the mentorship I was seeking, I had never before witnessed that level of commitment. My CEO is a man who lives the virtues. True leaders do not require titles. This is important for us all to examine when we go to the polls at election time.

I learned that night that you can not seek excellence and be afraid at the same time. The two cannot work together. My CEO demonstrated excellence even during the most difficult day of his career. The Mayor at that time showed fear and a lack of commitment to long term economic growth and the loss of the Games will have impacts on our community for decades. I had just left British Columbia where we were revitalizing impoverished neighbourhoods because of the 2010 Olympic and Paralympic Games. I had lived the excitement of major sporting events as catalysts for economic development. And yet, in the face of this tremendous loss, my CEO remained focussed upon raising funds and right action that day and remaining present to the needs of those around him. March 8th, 2007 remains forever etched in my mind for my CEO showed me what commitment looks like.

It is important to check in with yourself and ask yourself the following questions:

1. Does your current work/life situation allow you to think critically, independently and reflectively about the actions you take?

2. Are you able to follow your ethics in all that you do?

3. Are the people in your community in positions of political leadership demonstrating excellence and commitment?

I encourage you to take time out every day to check in on this until you can come to a point where you can answer "yes!" to these three questions. *Never* stop asking yourself these very important questions each and every day. And one day, what once allowed you to answer these questions with a "yes" may change. For the philosophers recognize that we are in a constant state of change and, therefore, it is important for us to consistently check in to ensure we are adapting to the changes around us in our lives, both professionally and personally.

Living in the present

We get into ruts when we live in the past. Marcus Aurelius, one of the greatest leaders of all time who led during war, strife and famine, wrote of people who carry "ghosts" around with them and that you can see these ghosts. What he meant by this is that these people are living in the past. They reference when life was good or they talk about what they used to have. These are people who have not adapted and moved forward.

It is never too late to begin to check in with yourself and ensure you are moving forward and not sliding into a rut and living in the past. People who are adapting and challenging and stretching themselves take risks in order to move forward. You will find an engaging, happy spirit about these people. There are no "ghosts" being carried about by people who are living and leading. For they are present.

Remember, everyone wondered why I could leave my company after six years to take a pay decrease and move to Nova Scotia. What seemed on the outside to be a strange decision for others was exactly what I needed to do to continue on my journey, my mission to obtain wisdom through the mentorship of great visionaries and to return home to invest in the place that shaped me. We have an expression in the East Coast of Canada, "Never forget where you came from." And by listening to my internal compass, I knew it was time to return home. When I made this decision I created a world filled with opportunities where others could not see them. I became excited and recharged about my work in new ways because I was being guided by my own internal compass.

And I returned home at a time when the economic outlook was grim, people were leaving in droves. To give you a comparison 90,000 people moved into the province of Alberta in 2006. That same year Nova Scotia lost 900 people. In times like these you gather the thought leaders and revitalize the economy so that we can better enlighten our aging voters on the importance of economic development to ensure there will be care providers for them and at the same time to ensure there are enough opportunties for youth to remain in the province to lead lives of meaning and opportunity.

Women leading by example

I have interviewed several women in this book who have a very joyous spirit. They have overcome the most incredible challenges to adapt, change and move forward. These women stretch themselves to live and lead authentically, regardless of what has been in their way. These women who live with philosophical direction have asked themselves the good questions about living ethically and authentically. These women are able to move forward in challenging times. From a mother who lost her son to bullying, to a mother who has to live thousands of miles from her children to build a better life for her babies, you will learn about these modern-day female philosophers and how they live the virtues in the following chapters. They have asked themselves the good questions that help them connect with their inner answers. This is known as the Socratic Method.

The Socratic Method

The unexamined life is not worth living.

– SOCRATES

The Socratic Method created by Socrates (399 AD) is a way of seeking the truest answer. It shows men and women how to think critically, independently and reflectively.

Socrates believed that humans had certain virtues. In his teachings he talked of how these virtues were the most important qualities we could have. Of these virtues, the philosophical and intellectual were the highest levels. Socrates really brought home the belief that virtues should be valued as your most precious possession. He taught that our ideal life should be spent seeking out the good life. Here's the challenge he would throw to you, the Philosopher Queen:

Your job is to find the truth beneath the shadows of existence and show others what the truth really is. Remember, decisions are made by those who show up. If you see things happening around you that are not leading to the good life, you must get engaged. And you will want to feel prepared when you show up by having the ability to ask the good questions.

The Socratic Method

• To argue logically

• To give and take a rational account

• To question and answer

It is important to note that the focus is using reason in your critical thinking, to ensure you are not relying on your senses. The senses can be fooled; reason can *not*.

When questioning and answering and in logical argument, never strip another person of their dignity. In a heated debate, emotion can creep in. Passion is a great thing when channeled effectively. However, remember to ensure that in your debate and desire to question, you do not get emotional which can lead to an indirect attack on one's dignity. Giving a person their dignity is the finest gift you can give and will take you further than any gift money can buy.

I have sat on several committees and boards. Whenever a diverse group of stakeholders gets together to guide an organization, conflicting perspectives can arise. I have witnessed this on several occasions and I am always amazed at the strength of the leader who does not get pulled into emotional dialogue, but rather stays calm and clear on the message. I recall one person who consistently challenged a project a committee of ours was working on. Nothing would satisfy him, not the stats nor the funding nor the profile could appease him. He felt that he should lead this project and would get so emotional that he would break out in a sweat and call people names. It was the most tragic display of a person incapable of using reason over emotion that I have ever witnessed. And it was fascinating to watch other men permit this man to behave in this manner.

I refused to validate this behaviour and held fast to my beliefs. It was not a very comfortable position, particularly when I would stand up to this person with the facts and he would continue to refuse to allow us to move forward. So I began to ask about this person to find out what the real agenda was. The facts should have been enough. "Why was he stalling progress?" I came to find out that he was planning on running for a council position and that he really wanted every opportunity to be seen as the fixer in the community and wanted to be seen as the leader.

So instead of unravelling or growing fearful of his illogical attacks, I would counter with logic every time. I was also able to change the policy on the committee selection for the following year to ensure only people with expertise in economic development and tourism would be permitted on the committee. This was an important lesson because it ensured people's time was respected and that those who wanted to pull progress off the rails because of hidden political agendas would not be allowed into the committee process. Those with expertise, and not an axe to grind would naturally want to move the process forward and add their expertise rather than slow the process down.

I have also observed people being played by others' agendas. This is very important because you do not want to be at the mercy of some-one else's hidden motives. I have witnessed people unraveling like a top when being pushed by others. It is so important that you ensure you maintain your dignity and at the same time, ensure you do not attack another person for having a different view.

> *Observe carefully what guides the actions of the wise, and what they shun or seek.*
>
> – MARCUS AURELIUS

Seek out ethical leaders in business and in government. They ensure that one's dignity is always maintained. I always tell young people– "Follow the smart people." They apply the Socratic Way.

The Socratic Way

Know thyself
Grow with friends
Ask great questions
Strengthen your soul
Verify everything
Speak frankly
Free your mind

> *All I have said about men applies equally to women.*
>
> – SOCRATES, *The Republic*

It is also important to note that Socrates, as recorded in his student Plato's famed work, *The Republic*, intended this way of thinking for women. Even though philosophy has not in the past been as ac-cesssible to women, it was always intended for us and it's never too late to become the Philosopher Queen you were intended to become.

What evidence is there that the shift from a patriarchal society has begun? When we are no longer in a patriarchal society, there will be no last names. Think of two of the most powerful women today– Madonna and Oprah.

The shift has begun.

In a patriarchal society, men enjoy certain privileges that are not extended to women.

I realized fully that the shift out of the patriarchal society had begun when I reconnected with the former President of King's College, Colin Starnes, who had come to give a lecture in Vancouver on the proposition that patriarchy had probably only begun some 6,000 years ago, shortly before the start of civilization. He suggested that, at least in the 'west', the conditions which had once encouraged its adoption had so changed that it was now irrevocably, (and for the most part unlamentedly), on its way out—even though the process would take a long time to complete.

And some of the growing pains of this shift out of the patriarchal society can be seen in every community. In Afghanistan you have the Taliban coming down hard because women are now connecting with their power. They are going to school and deciding they do not have to hide behind scarves if they do not wish to. It is their choice. The privileges men have over women are disappearing as women are becoming more independent.

To learn more about the patriarchy hypothesis and philosophy in general visit www.ukings.ca/kings_4055.html

So what will this shift from a patriarchal society look like for us and our generation? My prediction is that it will not privilege one gender or the other but harmonize both. The new emerging society will be a society where human beings, both male and female, have the ability to transcend gender stereotypes. All people will live beyond the patriarchal myth of women being tender and men being tough. The myth will no longer control us and people will be free to live authentically and perform right action, rather than simply fulfill cultural expectations. The starting point is to return to philosophy and build the foundations of your life or organization on the philosophical virtues. Through philosophical direction, I believe we can, as individuals, shift into this new model for a society where women are able to bridge the gap between rich and poor. *You* can be a part of making this shift.

The shift starts with each and every one of us stepping up and making a commitment to live the philosophical virtues in everthing we do.

**It is never too late to become what *you* envision for yourself.
Through the philosophical teachings in this book
you will learn:**

I   How to adopt an attitude of **Wonder** and gain
professional and personal advancement;

II How to obtain a strong and healthy mind, body
and spirit connection through the practice of
Moderation;

III How to avoid self-betrayal and find your own
Truth;

IV How to transform fear into **Courage**;

V   How to trust your instincts to ask the right questions
in the pursuit of **Justice**;

VI How to obtain the **Wisdom** needed to discover your
calling and life's purpose;

VII How to see the age-old view of true **Beauty** as the
result of balance and proportion in your life;

You already have the answers. Through the virtues,
now you can uncover them.

We learn best through self-discovery

– SOCRATES

The philosophers throughout history believed each of us is born knowing all the answers we need to lead lives of profound meaning. *The
7 Virtues of a Philosopher Queen* provides a modern take on the age-old
practice of seeking a life of meaning, both for ourselves as individuals
and for society. Through the *7 virtues* you are guaranteed not only to
get in touch with the answers within, but also to begin to live a far
more authentic life—the life you were meant to lead.

Philosophy itself is regarded as a male pursuit, and its norms of excellence are more often associated with men than women. It's time to revolutionize the benefits of philosophy for women. Historically, the study of philosophy or the humanities has been something reserved only for society's elite and those able to attend university.

Now there are programs such as the Clemente Program and Humanities 101 that are taking philosophy and the humanities to people living in the streets or in poverty and giving them the tools to advance their lives. The Clemente Program began when a university professor visited a woman in jail and asked what could have prevented her from going to prison. She said if she had only had a little bit of moral teaching, she would have made different choices. And the Clemente Program was born.

The dawning of educational outreach programs such as the Clemente Program and Humanities 101 have changed the lives of disadvantaged people for the better, by giving them the skills to choose right action. The successful record of accomplishment of these programs shows that philosophy and the study of the humanities is for *everyone*. These programs empower people living in poverty to focus upon the meaning of existence rather than simply existing. Those who endeavour to question, reflect and seek out answers to philosophical questions reap the benefits regardless of gender or socio-economic status. This is the key. Regardless of your gender or economic situation, a foundation of philosophical direction can take you to the highest levels of leadership and successful living.

By seeking to strengthen *The 7 Virtues*—**Wonder, Moderation, Truth, Courage, Justice, Wisdom** and **Beauty**—in your own life, you will uncover your own gifts. The secrets to obtaining a life of success and leadership have been before us for centuries, in male-coded teachings that have not been as accessible to women.

Through daily practice of the virtues you will learn how to strip away all the obstacles that keep you from leading your most meaningful life. The answers are all within us; we just need to free ourselves from the habits, practices and rules we've learned along the way that make us ineffectual. All of our lives we are trained to doubt and scrutinize ourselves instead of expressing our true nature. We spend our lives seeking the approval of others. Now it's time to trust ourselves.

Come back now to your sober senses; recall your true self;
awaken from slumber, and recognize that they were only dreams
that troubled you; and as you looked on them, so look now on
what meets your waking eyes.

– MARCUS AURELIUS

It is time to take philosophy out of the university classrooms and into our everyday lives. Through the help of philosophers and ordinary women who are living with a philosophical foundation, you will self-discover how philosophy can be applied to the world of modern women. *The 7 Virtues* are the foundation to living a successful life of meaning and purpose. Through the commitment to strengthen these virtues you will learn first hand what it means to live a philosophical life. I have included the stories of several women I have observed leading successfully and meaningfully in the face of challenges because they live philosophically. These real-life success stories alone warrant a modern take on the historic teachings.

The practice of living with philosophical direction accelerates the path to a life of leadership and meaning no matter what stage of your journey. It is never too late to become what you envision for yourself.

Philosophy is essential in uncovering a life of meaning and leadership. In *The 7 Virtues of a Philosopher Queen* you will find exercises that will assist you in uncovering your personal gifts that will enhance both your professional and personal life.

The results of your individual work based on *The 7 Virtues* will have an outstanding impact on the people in your life. In this book you will learn how to network with smart men and women to advance yourself as well as the people around you—for the Philosopher Queen is someone who connects her needs with those around her because she has uncovered her real purpose.

In the chapters ahead, you will learn how to harness the powers of philosophy to see the good in all challenges—this will empower you to "stay the course" in achieving personal and professional success. It is about choosing accountability and logic over emotion in moving forward with your work.

The shortest and surest way to live with honour in the world is to be in reality what we would appear to be; and if we observe, we shall find, that all human virtues increase and strengthen themselves by the practice of them.

- SOCRATES

VIRTUE

I

———

Wonder

I

Wonder rather than doubt is the root of knowledge.

– ABRAHAM JOSHUA HESCHEL

What is the first business of one who studies...To part with self conceit. For it is impossible for anyone to begin to learn what he thinks he already knows.

– EPICTETUS

When we allow ourselves to live the virtue of wonder, we are on the path of discovering the true reality of the world around us. When we make the choice to wonder instead of doubt, we immediately diverge and travel the path towards living with honour while allowing those around us to live with dignity.

Think back to a scenario where someone doubted you. That very situation would have obstructed communication between you and the other person. Regardless of what you need to achieve personally or professionally, doubt casts a shadow that immobilizes everyone concerned.

Now think back to a scenario where you doubted yourself and your own abilities. Pause and ask yourself what benefits you reaped from doubting yourself. I am quite certain there were no benefits in doubting your abilities. Ironically, we are taught to doubt ourselves all of our lives when trying to please others. When we doubt ourselves, we get further away from our own truths.

It is equally important that you keep an open mind—a mind of wonder—for the rest of your life. When we think we know everything, we close ourselves off from boundless opportunities and experiences. Socrates said, "I know nothing; therefore, I know something." It was this honest openness to wonder that led the great philosopher to teach and inspire people for thousands of years through the writings of his student, Plato.

Take the smartest person with the highest IQ who believes he or she knows everything and compare them with a person with a lesser IQ who has the capacity to wonder and is open to learning. The person with the lesser IQ will more than likely meet greater success. Yet we are taught to value the high IQ as it has become the "measure" in our status quo world. When we begin to value virtues such as wonder over status quo ideals that is when we begin to build healthier communities.

The best way to begin to apply the virtue of wonder is to apply Plato's allegory, or story of the cave. Plato was a great Greek philosopher. His famous allegory is really the "what if" scenario. It's the moment when we stop and ask ourselves, "I wonder what would happen if..."

Plato wrote *The Republic*, a book on politics, as he had a fascination with politics and sociology. In *The Republic* he wrote about the allegory of the cave. This allegory is still used today as an example of how we can better connect with our true world reality. The story is particularly valuable in our present-day society when sifting through the clutter of competing messages to gain perspective on reality. It is extra challenging to do this now more than ever with technology and messaging everywhere we go.

Plato's allegory of the cave is a parallel for our lives as humans and illustrates how we are not connected to the truth. In the allegory Plato said that it would take the Philosopher King (as he referred to men) and from now on we'll use the word Philosopher Queen—to break away and find the courage to seek the truth. Long before truth comes the virtue of wonder. That is where we will begin.

Plato's allegory of the cave

Plato's allegory of the cave is a famous story told for over 2,000 years. It demonstrates that we, as humans, regardless of the point in history or modern times, are not truly living our own authentic lives. Plato showed us it takes Philosopher Queens and Kings to seek out the truth so that we can live authentically and successfully.

The allegory of the cave tells the story of prisoners (representing humanity) who have been chained to the walls of a cave since they were children. The sun is outside the cave and is very bright. The prisoners do not look into the sun (a symbol for the truth) but look instead at the flickering shadows cast inside the cave. The prisoners believe these shadows to be their reality, the world around them. In truth, the shadows are not the real objects but the shadows of the objects passing by inside the cave.

It takes the Philosopher Queen to wonder about the shadows she is living in and to seek ways to uncover her true reality.

Here is the challenge

The Philosopher Queen who challenges the status quo and seeks out her true reality will find it difficult, as it is challenging, and sometimes painful, to uncover the truth. Once she has found the truth by looking into the sun, she now has to go back and convince the prisoners living in the shadows that what they are living is not the truth. In Plato's allegory, these prisoners represent much of humanity. The chains that bind them to the cave are symbols of the things that influence us such as media, family and society: all of the outside influences that steer us in the direction *they* believe we should be going.

In effect, the allegory of the cave shows us that we are living not knowing the truth. Plato goes on to explain that the Philosopher Kings and Queens—the men and women who have freed themselves, will try to help the prisoners to unchain themselves so that everyone can discover the truth.

However, there are guards in the cave and they represent authority figures who wish to keep people in a state that supports their authoritarian power. This we will discuss further in the chapter on **Courage** and how important it is to get more Philosopher Queens in positions of leadership in government, business and media. That is the ultimate objective of our journey as women—to reconnect with our power—not hand it over.

The cave where the prisoners are is symbolic for our bodies. Plato believed that our bodies keep us from seeing our true reality as they keep us concentrating on material things. Think about how much energy we waste worrying about our weight, hair, clothes or keeping up with the Joneses.

The test

The Philosopher Queen's goal is to get beyond what is irrelevant and connect with what really matters—enabling her to find success and true life meaning. Plato taught that the sun (symbolic for the truth) is kept from shining upon us (our souls) because our true souls are trapped inside the cave (our bodies). Plato wrote that if our souls could exit the cave—meaning that if we place a higher value on reason and the spirit than on the physical—we would then be able to see our true reality.

Breaking the chains of society's expectations and really connecting with the truth is no easy task. Once the prisoner breaks the chains, she is able to leave the cave as a Philosopher Queen and allow the bright light of the sun to illuminate what is really happening around her. In leaving the cave she casts off all the teachings and manipulation imposed throughout her life by her parents, society and culture—false messages that have kept her from living her true life plan. Most people, both men and women, are unable to break the chains as it's too frightening to go against the cultural norms and expectations of others. They remain merely content in living safe, unexamined lives with no desire to stretch for the light. The result is a life spent in a state of dissatisfaction about their lives—that "something's missing" feeling—whether it be professional or personal. These people are also at the mercy of others who deploy them.

When we do not live and lead with our own philosophical dirction and convictions, we run a higher risk of being swayed and manipulated by the motives of others. Look at how in debt North America is. That debt can be tracked back to the influence of society and advertising, convincing people their lives would be better if they spent more money. And the endless cycle of spending in the quest for hapiness ensues—sadly to never be satisfied—since things cannot make one happy.

It is the Philosopher Queen who can see what is really happening in the world around her because the sun lights the way. The challenge the Philsosopher Queen will take on is to return to talk with the prisoners (humanity) and explain the truth she has seen. Hardly anyone will listen to her because the prisoners don't understand the new, enlightened language she has learned as their language is limited to what's inside the cave.

Language is the key

Language is an important part of how we become true Philosopher Queens. We must test out, examine and be persistant in our desire to communicate the truth to others. We must never stop examining the language used in historically male-dominated worlds such as business and government. Understanding that language is key to communicating the path to truly enlightened living. For if you have a message and are able to communicate it to predominately male leaders in government and business, you will move your goals and causes forward through fostering understanding and support, ultimately earning the attention your work deserves.

While living in British Columbia, I wrote a column called "The Good Life." The process itself had me examining the three levels of government, non-profit and the private sector working together to build a healthy society. When I moved to Halifax, within a few months I began writing a column called "Culture Shift" in the business section of The Chronicle Herald on connecting the benefits of economic development to our every day lives. This is where I hone my skills on being brave and speaking the truth in the language that people understand. So it is important for each of us to find our own ways to learn the language of the worlds of business and government if we wish to bring about real change in our society.

If you will look into the "light" with me for a moment, I would like to share some things with you that I believe we can reverse. And if you think these things are irreversible—remember, the philosophers believe we have every resource available to us to lead a life of meaning, that we have everything we need to make big, dramatic and positive changes in society. We can reverse the following challenges through a foundation in philosophical thinking.

Consider how illogical the world is:

• One in five children lives in poverty in North America
and yet women aged 35-55 hold the buying power. We
must harness this buying power to reverse the cycle of
poverty.

• Of the top 500 CEOs in Canada, only 19 are women.
Yet women are the fastest growing group of self-employed
entrepreneurs. We have the skills yet we are not making
the top decisions that have significant impacts on society.

• In politics, 52 per cent of the voting power in North
America is in the hands of women and yet we have only
20 per cent representation by women in political seats.
We own the voting power and are giving it away.

• The diet industry has grown into a billion dollar
industry. Yet North Americans have never been heavier.
The culture of instant gratification is resulting in
significant debt and excess.

Plato went on to explain that because the prisoners (humanity) in the
cave have not experienced the "light" they cannot understand the
truth because they have no language for the divine. When you think
about the challenges cited above, this puts our illogical world into
context and makes it clear that it's time for us to assume leadership to
make the changes we need for equal representation in business and
government. It also shows us the need to move our attentions towards
reason and logic instead of investing in an unhealthy focus on body
image.

We only have so much energy to focus our attentions on our work
and goals. Reflect upon where your energy is going and if it is going
to good use.

For those of us living in the cave, in the shadows, in order to understand the Philosopher Queen's message, we must begin to at least
"loosen" the chains that bind us by questioning what advertisers, media,
our family and authority figures tell us is the truth. And we must also
begin to learn the language of the philosophers so that when a Phil-

osopher Queen comes to share the truth with us, we will understand her language and not miss the message.

Importance of learning the language

If the issues that rest with narrowing the gap between poverty and wealth can be found in the worlds of business and government, then women need to learn the language that historically has dominated these arenas. If we are to deliver a message of truth, then we need to be speaking the same language.

The philosophers tell us that it does not matter whether it's 40 years or 40 thousand years—humanity is the same.

> *Look back over the past, with its changing empires that rose and fell, and you can foresee the future too. Its pattern will be the same, down to the last detail; for it cannot break step with the steady march of creation. To view the lives of men for forty years or for forty thousand is therefore all one; for what more will there be for you to see?*

> – MARCUS AURELIUS

Unless we begin to learn from the past, we will be doomed to live out the same mistakes over and over. Plato wrote over 2,000 years ago and his allegory of the cave applies today as much as it did back then. Humanity is the same; our issues and challenges simply manifest themselves differently throughout time.

When I give talks on visualization to high school youth today, I see that young people feel many of the same pressures that my generation felt back in the mid-eighties. I remind them that drag-racing BMWs may be a peer pressure-influenced activity now, but back in my time, Mike the Ram was pretty popular at the county fair tractor-pulls. The students laugh. Seriously, that was an event not to be missed and when I think of being 15 at that event, I knew there were pressures all around me. Fortunately, I was not part of the "cool" crowd, so I did not get drawn into the material issues that can burden youth. That message resonates with young people. By the end of the talk, most of the room has acknowledged that they, too, are *nerds* and my message to them is this: you are the leaders of tomorrow—continue to march to your own beat.

Finally, the cave in Plato's allegory has become a metaphor for the way mass media dominates public understanding and comes between us as individuals and the meaning of events to our own lives.

I recall my professor of Journalism Ethics, Bruce Wark, telling us that if you really want to know what is happening in your own back-yards, simply open the back door and take a look for yourself. In other words, ensure that you are using your own powers of observation and not relying on other people's interpretations. Ensure that you are forming your own reasoning skills and educating yourself to have a better sense of what is really happening around you and how events impact your life in real ways.

I literally go outside and stand in my backyard every so often just to look around and remind myself of what is really going on. I also have my ear to the ground and travel throughout the community speaking with people in business, government and non-profit sectors to find out what is happening on the streets.

Socrates felt that women should come to a place where we value giv-ing birth to our ideas as much as we value giving birth to our children. Men certainly do. It is important that women begin to cherish and hone the ability to reason as one of our most precious attributes, far superior to looks, height, or the fashion of the day. And it begins with **Wonder**. Our goal is not to doubt the influences around us, but to wonder and reason.

> *Virtue can only flourish among equals.... In fact, it is a farce*
> *to call any being virtuous whose virtues do not result from the*
> *exercise of its own reason.*
>
> – MARY WOLLSTONECRAFT

To wonder is to reason. And reason will help you discover the truth about yourself and your place in the world. It's time to become the kind of Wonder Woman who will use reason to take yourself and the people in your life forward.

No one can teach you how to become yourself. Only you can. Some people are fortunate to find a clear path in their youth and others recreate themselves mid-life. Life is a continuous journey, a lifetime process of *becoming.*

The Philosopher Heraclites believed that everything is always changing and that we must adapt to that change in order to be in the *flow.* It does not matter where you are in your process of self-discovery, as long as you are able to let go of the past and move forward.

Fulfilling our potential is the ultimate goal.

> *The opinion of 10,000 men is of no value if none of them knows anything about the subject.*
>
> – MARCUS AURELIUS

To gain true knowledge we must separate ourselves from people who merely hold opinions. Therefore, we need to learn. We realize that we must learn new things to make new experiences. And to educate yourself you need to ask questions. This is not a standard held only by the elite. Through the exercises in this book, anyone can reach a place of knowledge and self-direction.

There are current programs such as the Clemente Program and Humanities 101 that teach people who are disadvantaged to reflect through the readings of philosophers. These people are now transforming their lives by asking themselves questions about "The Good Life." This proves that every one of us has the power to use philosophy as the foundation for self-discovery.

Some of the world's greatest leaders were self-taught, educating themselves by reading the great philosophers. Winston Churchill comes to mind right away.

Sir Winston Churchill—the great leader

Churchill was one of the greatest leaders of all time. Yet in his youth, he was a mediocre student with a strong desire to lead. He took on challenges to learn first-hand how to achieve his goal. He studied the works of the great philosophers on his own. He read Plato, Socrates, and the other greats to develop his own capacity to reason. With this skill, he was able to apply philosophical reasoning to real-life situations. Even when the world seemed to be against him, he did not take it personally. He forged ahead with his mission and ended WWII—ultimately saving the world.

Churchill used knowledge over opinion.

Because of his philosophical direction, Churchill was able to do the *right* thing, regardless of what people thought of him. If you read up on Churchill, you will find that at certain points in history, many people loathed him. In the end, after the famous Victory Day speech, he was adored the world over, so much so that a girl living in Mexico wrote a letter to "The Greatest Man in the World."

That letter found its way to Churchill.

Sir Winston Churchill is a very important example of a person who demonstrated philosophical thinking through every challenge imaginable. He is an example of how philosophical direction guided our world to freedom—think about this and its application to today's world situation. Churchill was also an artist and a great orator. He practiced in his mind how to be eloquent and to move people to action.

There was another person who did the same thing during his day—Adolph Hitler, the power-hungry Nazi dictator. Hitler misled many people who were unaware of his sinister plot to annihilate an entire race and take over the world. Churchill could see through this. Using knowledge based on philosophical thinking, Churchill was able to see the truth. His challenge as a Philosopher King was to then communicate the truth to the people which he did through a great deal of time and effort invested in speech writing so that he could use the language the people needed to hear to understand the truth and to move them to right action. Listen to a recorded Churchill speech or speak with someone who lived in the day and you will understand the power of the language needed to enlighten people during challenging times.

Let's go back in time for a moment; imagine the time period in which Churchill lived. Socialites were being wooed by Hitler's charm. When a Harvard-educated Hitler associate called Churchill to invite him to lunch, most people of the day would have leaped at the chance. Remember, Hitler was very controlling and had brainwashed people easily, since most of them were living in the shadows of the cave and could not formulate right action.

When Hitler's associate called Churchill to arrange the lunch, he tried to charm him as he'd charmed others by saying, "You and Hitler will get along great—you are both lovers of the Arts and great orators." Churchill simply asked this one important question: "What does Hitler think of the Jewish People?"

The lunch never happened.

Churchill valued human life over power and chose to follow right action regardless of the opinion of the day. He then set about ensuring that the Nazis would not take over Europe.

Churchill was able to put right action for the greater good before his own desires for power. Now this is very important to reflect upon.

This is where a great leader emerges

By asking the right questions and following right action, you will *ultimately* meet success. It is not easy. It was not easy for Churchill, but it was well worth it to save modern-day civilization. Recall the allegory of the cave. The Philosopher Queen will need to look into the light (truth) and bring that message back to everyone else. Winston Churchill asked the right questions and saw the truth, shedding the light on evil. We all have that power.

When we say a leader emerges, the leader is already inside of each one of us. We all have the capacity to ensure we do the right thing when called upon in everyday leadership no matter what challenges we may face.

Now we enter a world of blurred lines when it comes to our own world state. Many people are saying, "We need another Churchill." You need look no further than yourself. Each one of us can ask the right questions to serve the greater good and those around us by understanding *The 7 Virtues* and incorporating philosophical thinking into our everyday lives.

Success is the ability to go from failure to failure without losing your enthusiasm

– WINSTON CHURCHILL

The virtues of **Wonder, Moderation, Truth, Courage, Justice, Wisdom** and **Beauty** are non-partisan and they are bound by no organized religion. With philosophical direction, we can strip away all of the negative or opinionated judgments we were taught culturally. With Philosophical direction you can ensure you are no longer controlled by others and can feel good about the decisions *you* make.

The Virtues in our everyday lives

Begin to Wonder—a creative surge

The definition of creativity is to think in the opposite way you would normally think. And since creativity is valued throughout society as a means of finding solutions in difficult situations, as a leader it's crucial to either become a *creator* or at least embrace those around you who are able to come up with creative solutions to challenges.

The first step to creativity—or "thinking in the opposite way you would normally think" is to *wonder*.

You begin to ask, "What if?"

There is nothing dangerous or frightening about wondering *what if.* Veer off and ask yourself the *what if* questions about your current work challenges or your life in general. This process is necessary to get to the answers within.

When you think of the most creative people who have graced the earth: Michelangelo, Einstein, and, in modern times, Madonna and Oprah, I can guarantee they stopped and asked themselves *what if.*

The allegory of the cave is all about asking yourself "What if I…" and to resist the constraints of the chains which symbolize all the things that taught you along the way that you could not do something. Wonder allows us to cast off the chains that have bound us by our culture. To wonder is the first step to rid yourself of any negative thoughts that made you believe you were capable of less than you were made for.

It was through the feeling of wonder that men now and at first began to philosophize.

– ARISTOTLE

Let's begin the journey of *I wonder*.

Here are a few "I wonder" statements that I have asked myself which have led to some of the most incredible results. After you read them, take a bit of time to jot down a few "I wonder" statements for your own life and then take action on them.

To give you an idea of what kinds of I wonder statements that will work best for you, think of the things that you feel may be stopping you from advancing in your personal and professional life.

Here are my "I wonder" statements:

- I wonder what would happen if I started taking golf lessons?

- I wonder what would happen if I invited the CEO of a large company out for lunch?

- I wonder what would happen if I started my own company?

- I wonder what would happen if I said no thank you to my family when they offer me food I don't want to eat?

- I wonder what would happen if I took some time out of every day to do exercises that I like?

- I wonder what would happen if I took some time to reflect each day to understand what my life's work should be?

The virtue of wonder can take you on journeys you'd never imagined possible right in the comfort of your own home, while commuting in your car, on the bus to work, while washing the dishes, or working out.

The challenge in life is ensuring you are not stuck in a rut. Should you find yourself in a rut, these "I wonder" statements are the first step guaranteed to move you forward.

My favourite place to reflect and wonder has always been on an airplane or on the water. I have found that being above the clouds or on the water, connected to nature's vastness, is an amazing way to think with clarity. It is the clutter of messages from others that keeps us from connecting to the answers we already have within.

Another very productive way to think is to do something manual. When I poured coffee at the airline, or washed the dishes, the act of doing something with my hands somehow allowed my mind to slow down and I would go into a natural reflective state.

Ask yourself where and what situations naturally put you in a reflective state. Now add the "I wonder what if" statement to your thoughts and dare to think in the opposite way you would normally think to get the creative process moving. Wonder will take you out of a rut and into brave new territory in your mind. That's where all great decisions begin.

To wonder is to ask great questions of yourself–and *that* is philosophy in action!

By asking great questions of yourself, you will be pleasantly surprised at the clear answers you may already have within.

I asked myself all of the questions listed above. Here are some stories about the bold, successful territory the virtue of wonder has enabled me to conquer in my personal and professional life. These are real-life examples of stretching myself through the virtues rather than looking upon challenges or situations with a doubtful approach or an approach influenced by others. This is key to living your best life.

A colleague of mine in BC took our mayor out golfing and they invited my female mentor and excluded me because I did not golf. Instead of feeling shut out, I said to myself, *I wonder what would happen if I started taking golf lessons?*

I was 34 years old and had no depth perception–I could not even hit the ball. I called up all the women in business I knew, and we hired a young, patient, fun golf pro to teach us. Now, not only are many of my connections made on the golf course, but I have also engaged a whole group of women who had previously found themselves on the fringe.

When I asked Peter Legge, CEO of Canada Wide Media Limited, out to lunch, he said yes. Although I wanted to ask him about politics and business, what I received was inspiration to write this book. Peter has written seven books including *The Runway of Life,* and *I Wish I'd Said That.* Peter is a motivational speaker in North America and ranked at the top by Toast Masters International. It just so happens that we lived in the same town in British Columbia and I would see him a lot at functions and fundraisers. In fact, our first conversation was about a book we had both read—*The Tipping Point.* Peter reads one book a week. I also had the honour of working with Peter on establishing the Peter Legge Library, which is the only motivational book library in Canada.

When I told Peter that I wanted to write this book for women, he said, "Barb, take an empty book and wrap the cover of your book around it. Place it on your desk and use that visualization to ensure you complete the book."

You would not be enjoying this book if I had not asked myself, *I wonder what would happen if I invited the CEO of a large company out to lunch?*

When I was the writer/producer for a technology TV show, I had grown frustrated that we could not completely guide our clients on the challenges in the business world of the day. So one day when I was telling the head of Sales that there was an opportunity to work with another large company and that I knew the Chief Operating Officer (COO), he looked down at me in my cubicle and asked me how I could know the COO. He was in such disbelief that he never even bothered to follow up with him. I then gave the contact information to the senior female producer who jumped in her car and drove down to meet my contact. They did great business and I said to myself, *I wonder, what would happen if I started my own company?*

I realized that my intelligence and skill at relationship building was not being recognized and as a result, I would never hone my skills. So I decided to leave the company.

There had been other instances while working for this show that I felt the work would ultimately compromise my ethics, so I gave my two-weeks notice and left the show. I took a one year program at a local college on entrepreneurship. Two weeks before I graduated, the college hired me to do their marketing. From there I launched my company, Acclimatize Communications Corp., and tripled my salary by staying true to my values and ethics. And it all began with a simple *I wonder.*

I learned a very important lesson from the head of Sales. I learned that my word and my self-respect are worth more than a pay-cheque. This experience gave me the confidence to move on and the rewards were significant.

I was a very large, overweight child growing up. By the time I was 15, I had reached 210 pounds. Our family loved to eat, and I realized that this was not healthy. Although I had not been exposed to healthy eating or exercise, I knew these were things I could create for myself. So I asked myself, *I wonder what would happen if I said no thank you when my family offers me more food than I need?*

Do you know what happened? I lost 60 pounds before returning to high school. I simply ate less and walked for two hours every day. Anyone who has ever lost weight knows that this is a life-long challenge. And so, in the chapter on **Moderation**, I will share with you what I have done to keep the weight off for over 20 years. The virtues are the fastest way to advance your life in the direction you choose. You know what is good for your life, and by practicing the virtue of wonder, you will get that much closer to your goals.

The virtue of wonder is the first step to living and leading in an illogical world

In my hectic work day I realized that all of a sudden, exercise had taken a back seat to work. When you circle with other A-type personalities, there is a cultural pressure to work hard. And it's not until you step back and realize that you could work 24/7 and still never be finished, you really see how important it is to take time out to exercise. It was during the height of my work pace that I stopped and asked myself, *I wonder what would happen if I took time out every day to do exercises that I like?*

Studies have shown that managers who work out are more apt to get the promotions. I'm not sure if it's because they have the physical confidence from working out each day or if it's the added insight that a workout provides. Most fit people agree that they find answers to questions that have eluded them when they turn their minds off to exercise. And again, there is that manual thing, where you are moving your body and your mind enters a reflective state as you follow the mechanics of the work-out. This allows your subconscious to work out many of the hard questions that were challenging you. Turning off your mind during a workout allows the answers that you already have within to surface. Again, this is proof that the answers to all of your questions are already inside of you. The endorphins produced by working out also relieve the stress of a hectic lifestyle—they give you a natural high and make you happy. We all gravitate towards people who are happy because they feel good about themselves and make us feel good. These people are more apt to meet success because everyone wants to be a part of what they are doing. This also reveals the connection between the mind, body and spirit. Answers come to you through the movement of your body. Exercising your body, in effect, exercises your mind.

How do you find the time to work out? Cancel your cable if need be. Absolutely get rid of anything that is a big time waster in *your* life if you have any challenge finding the time to work out. It's been said that those who are living are on TV and those who are simply on the outside watching others live are watching TV. For women, particularly those with young children, we don't have much time—so we have to maximize it. This may sound harsh, but it's been proven that household income goes up 50 per cent when the TV is removed from the living room. Now this doesn't mean you have to give up TV—it's merely a starting point to reflect upon. I wonder what would happen if I cancelled the cable for one month? What benefits would our family reap? You can always subscribe again if you miss it. I cancelled our cable when I launched my company and my income tripled. I knew that I was wasting time watching other people live and I chose to be a doer.

You have just 16 waking hours in the day. It's important to prioritize just what it is that you want and what you need to do to get it. Eighty per cent of our thoughts can be negative, and this has been attributed to the barrage of media images and messages in our daily lives. By canceling our cable in 2001, I have added hours to my day and yet I miss nothing. I get my news online, I read *Oprah* Magazine when I commute or when waiting for an appointment. Ensure you are in control of the thoughts and influences that enter your mind. By controlling your media, you are, in effect, controlling your outcomes.

I am controlling my media and in effect controlling my outcomes

My solution to exercise is to work out for one hour every morning between 6:00 and 7:00 a.m., when no one is up and the world doesn't need me. I go to bed every night at 8:30 or 9:00 pm. There's nothing going on then either and there's no TV show to distract me from getting a good night's sleep. Most meetings are finished by this time of night and should I stay up late for an evening on the town, I still get up for my workout. Taking the time for my workout every day is one of the most important gifts I can give to myself—I call it "paying myself first."

When you see the chapter on **Moderation**, we will discuss Plato's tripartite soul. This is where true happiness is the result of the three parts of the soul acting in harmony. The three parts are reason, the spirit and the body. Only you will know what the perfect balance is between your intellectual, spiritual and physical makeup. Know that the start of discovering this harmony is to give attention to all three every day to ensure you are on your way to leading a balanced life. Let none of the three take over fully, but give reasonable attention to each.

I do not have, nor do I wish to have, a so called "perfect" body. It is just not a priority. And even though our culture may dictate that we should be made to strive towards this, the philosophically directed mind can ignore these distractions. I do, however, want to feel strong and keep my good posture into my older years, and for those reasons I work out with no expectation of a perfect body. Since my expectations are clearly set out, I cannot be swayed to think otherwise. I work out every day. Every day I work different muscles for balance. I feel strong, confident and healthy and there is a certain beauty in all of that coming together.

It was the ancient Greeks who mastered philosophy and the healthy balance of sport and fitness into their lives. Think of the Olympics as the perfect combination of body, mind and spirit connected to reach a goal. There's a philosophy to the sport mind. The word "coach" in Life Coach was inspired by the techniques coaches in sport used to motivate and challenge athletes to reach their peak performance and to lead in their chosen field.

As I began to give my talks on visualization to youth, I realized that I was talking about leadership and how at the end of the day, it's normal for me to sit with other leaders. The work I do in economic development and service and in volunteerism impacts the lives of those around me. This led me to realize that my work has got to be meaningful and that it must make positive change. Raised by a single mom, I often have the single mom and her children in my thoughts. How we manage the growth of our cities and the importance of ensuring they are safe and that citizens have access to opportunities to advance their own lives is a priority of mine.

I said to myself, *I wonder what would happen if I took some time to reflect each day to understand what my life's work should be?* I choose to do this right after my workouts in the morning, at 7:00 am when no one is up yet. This gives me 30 minutes to read philosophy books and reflect on how I will go about my day. It was through this reflection time that I realized many things about myself and—most importantly—I connected with that inner voice that is so hard to hear during the clutter of our busy days. After doing this over many months, I began to realize there was a book inside of me. This was an incredible discovery and I have grown from having to work towards taking this time—to craving it.

It was during these reflections that it dawned on me how crucial it is for women to connect and do the work we were put on this earth to do. Recognizing that we still live in a patriarchal world, I would like to focus upon the importance of doing business in a predominantly male-coded business world.

> *I do not wish [women] to have power over men; but over themselves.*
>
> – MARY WOLLSTONECRAFT

Mary Wollstonecraft wrote *A Vindication of the Rights of Woman* in the 1700s. It was in reading her book that I said to myself, *I wonder if I could try and crack the old boys' code and open the door to today's woman by learning their language and then explaining it to my peers?*

It has been said that women are not able to rise to the top in large corporations or in politics in equal numbers as men because of our lack of networks. The network is also a timely subject as the top futurist in North America, Faith Popcorn, had forecasted that the "Network" would be the top trend for 2007. Popcorn nailed it. In an age of technology with Facebook and blogs, the potential for building your network has expanded in new ways. However, there are still powerful networks such as business and government that use networking in ways that have historically not been utilized as much by women. As a rule, women do not hang out on golf courses or discuss sports or the TSE at social clubs. Men *do*. Men build networks based on a long-established language that permits entry into these networks. The power to advance personally and professionally is held in great part by these networks of people.

I was watching a political debate on CNN the other day while I was in a hotel for a conference. There were three men and one woman discussing the U.S. election. They were all equally intelligent and equally respectful and enlightening. However, when one of the gentlemen likened a presidential candidate to an agent discovering a baseball player, it hit me: it really is language—a predominantly male language—that encompasses competition, perfecting a craft, leadership and fun. So instead of seeing his comment as a male comment about sports bordering on exclusion, I realized that this was his language and that his reference was not unlike a word or phrase in a language new to me. And that we, as women, can set about to do the work to understand this new language so that we can participate fully with men in business, politics, and yes, sports.

The language of sports

If we look at sports and how they have shaped men and women, we see that healthy competition and self-challenge are key. That is not to say that you have to run out and become a sports fanatic, but it is important to examine athletic competition and the language behind it. Good sportsmanship demonstrates the ability to lose with grace and dignity. The ability to try harder next time and learn from our losses is equally important. Sports teach us to cheer someone on. All of this translates into every aspect of our lives.

Team work is a natural component of sports and a phrase used commonly in the workplace. If you have never been on a sports team, you may want to either join one (it is never too late) or take an interest in observing sports as a fan. With the importance of networks that include everyone, particularly in economic development in communities, it is crucial for us to begin to see the interests of the whole rather than just our own. Sports help us to see the world this way.

I was never on a sports team growing up. In university, because I am fairly tall at over 5 feet 9 inches, I was asked to join the rowing team. What an experience! We had our moments as we were all adapting to each other in the first days—if all rowers are not moving in synch with each other the boat will either tip, crash or not move at all. But when we did move together in one rhythm with a shared goal to get to the finish line first, it was the most amazing feeling.

Keep your eyes in the boat

We were taught not to look outside of the boat at the other boats coming up the side because that would distract us from our goal of working as one to win the race. This is interesting for us in our work. In philosophical thinking, we are taught not to concern ourselves with what others are doing or saying because this will distract us from our own purpose.

Our rowing team knew our purpose: to stay unified, to work together to get to the finish line first. If a rower began to look outside the boat, they risked being psyched out by the competing boats and we would not have reached our unified goal.

To make matters even more interesting, our team arrived at the competing school for the rowing finals dressed in cut-off jeans, with ancient wooden boats that should have been in a museum.

The other teams were wearing spandex and had state-of-the-art fiberglass boats with microphone systems to communicate. We thought that was impressive, but never did we think they were better than us.

For us, the measure was never material, but in skill. Besides, we knew how to sing in harmony and had shirts that said, "Not tonight...I have to row." Everyone wanted our shirts, so we sold them as a fundraiser.

The point is that we never wavered in our faith in our abilities—our goals were solid and clear and we could not be psyched out. Yes, we won our races. And yes, we were students of philosophy.

Learning the language of healthy competition

So what if you could begin to understand this language used for centuries in a male-dominated culture of government and business?

You would become one of the most networked and requested women recognized by both genders as a leader and an authority on your work.

A good way to check in to see if you are in this network or not, is to write down the names of the men in business or politics that you could call right now if you needed to get something done for your place of work, community group or your kids' school.

If you are able to come up with at least 10-15 male CEOs from the business and/or political world, then you're in. If you are unable to come up with 10-15 names, then know that you're not alone. Women leaders are usually the CEOs of non-profit organizations more than private sector businesses. This noble role is crucial to society, but who is she going to call for assistance if the private sector and government leaders are predominantly male and she hasn't built a relationship with them so that they can work together? Women are also the fastest growing group running small businesses, which is a very exciting shift. However, often the small business is not connected to the major power sources which can influence decisions that impact the divide between rich and poor.

At this stage I would like to add that the fabric crucial to a successful society includes healthy relationships between all levels of government, non-profit and the private sector, with shared goals on the advancement of society. Keep in mind the fact that one in five children lives in poverty in our wealthy western society. That is, in the end, what we intend to resolve, taking the steps to advance our lives personally and professionally along the way.

Women's groups—on the *fringe* of the power base

When I was an advisor to business start-ups in Vancouver, British Columbia, I advised my clients to look for the right networking group for their business. With the broad range of groups out there, it was definitely the part of the business process that caused the most confusion and anxiety. Spending money to join a group that may not be the right fit on top of having to enter a room where people may not accept or embrace you naturally was frightening for these people who were new to business. Chambers, Boards of Trade, Women in Business, golf clubs, social clubs, hockey clubs, and tennis clubs—the list goes on. I advised my clients to target a few groups that looked promising, attend a few sessions without committing to a long-term membership, and ask yourself what works for *you*.

If you are nervous about entering a place where you do not know anyone, remember what philosopher Marcus Aurelius would tell you—that we are not put on this earth to invest energy in worrying about what others may think of us. We are here to define our own path and connect with our own higher purpose. It is important to keep this uppermost in your mind when you feel the slide into valuing what's not relevant.

Philosophical tips for entering a room

1. We will no longer be living in 100 years—so who cares what someone thinks of you? One hundred years from now, will anyone care that you attended a networking event and entered a room where you did not know anyone? No—so get on with it.

2. Why would you invest any energy in worrying about others' opinions of your direction when they do not necessarily know what their own purpose is in life?

3. Be clear on your goals to advance to the next level. There could be someone at that event willing to help you with your goals, but how will you meet that potential contact if you do not attend?

4. People love self-directed people. Walk in, head high,

with a clear visualization of how the event will work out. Read up on the subject matter and as soon as you sign in, begin to ask interesting questions—*that* is the key. The philosopher asks engaging questions of herself and of others.

Suggested Questions to ask others:

• I read about the speaker tonight—have you read her book yet?

• This is my first time here; have you been to one of these networking sessions before?

• I decided to come and see what this group is about because I'm thinking of joining. Why did you choose this group? What do you find valuable about being a part of this group?

• I was a little nervous to come here alone at first, but now that I've met people like you, I think I may join. What can this group offer me?

The definition of charisma—a humble confidence

Think about charismatic people. The people that everyone wants to be around have a quality that we refer to as charisma. These are *not* people who try to please everyone.

People who have a presence have a humble confidence

It is the Philosopher Queen that has to strip away her ego completely and be humble. At the same time, her soul is balanced with mind, body and spirit all connected in harmony. For that, she is sought after. Interestingly, she only cares to be sought after so that she can be heard by others in order to do her work. In other words, she has built a way of being and speaks a language that empowers her to deliver the truth, and the people in the "cave" listen to her. So when you see someone who just stops the room and causes everyone to look up, not for beauty but for her ability to reason and help others, you are standing in the presence of a Philosopher Queen. And often there is an inner beauty or light that the Philosopher Queen gives off–that humble confidence known as charisma.

That is our work in this book. We wish to become Philosopher Queens so that we can do our work on this earth and build *The Good Life* for ourselves and those around us.

Bridging the gap

I am often asked to speak on economic development and the most memorable engagements were to women's business groups. Now, these events were memorable because these women asked the greatest questions that related to children and society, but unfortunately, these women were not necessarily connected to the power source. So essentially, they were halfway there in making the connection between rich and poor. They had not yet accessed the power sources–the networks of top men in business and government. That last crucial step is what I focus on in my talks.

I will never forget the time I gave a talk to a group of women in business on Vancouver Island. There were about 90 women who wanted to know more about opportunities stemming from the 2010 Vancouver Olympic Games, for both their community and their own businesses. I spoke with the organizer and we got to know each other over the phone, talking about our kids and work, and the focus of the presentation I would make. I prepared by working with my friend, Brian Krieger, the General Manager of the 2010 Commerce Centre, who worked on procurement with local businesses for the Olympic and Paralympic Games.

What played out before and after the session is what fascinated me about how we, as women, have far to go in building our networks–and at the same time, these same women showed me something equally important about the role of women in the next generation coming up. In essence, we taught each other something very big that I will explain in the next few pages.

In the planning stages of the event, I recommended to the organizer that another friend of mine, their city's Manager of Economic Development, John Watson, should attend the session to connect the women in business with local initiatives. I was told no, this person was a man, and this networking session was for women only. *Wow* I thought, here we are doing what we dislike most about men's groups—shutting someone out because of gender. So I invited him anyway.

I never told John that he was not invited, as I figured I could persuade the women's business group to reconsider. And as luck would have it, a couple of days before the event, the organizer called and said he could come.

When I arrived I read the local newspaper. I learned about their economic issues and saw some very real ways these women could make economic change in their community that could have lasting positive impacts on children, seniors, and on their own businesses.

And so the session began. We enjoyed dinner and then I was presented. The organizer got up and instead of introducing my talk right away, she got emotional and spoke about learning from our telephone conversations how to bond with her young son by having lunch at his school once a week, one on one. I had shared with her that this was my way of ensuring that my son and I remain connected during my hectic work life, that I could see who his friends were, and that they could also observe that it's quite cool for a son and his mom to be close. I started this ritual when I thought there was a bit of bullying going on by his peer group and wanted to show them in a kind way that I am present, nearby, and very much find my son to be engaging.

Now as she spoke of this, I realized I could have talked more on this subject, but I was there to get down to business. What I have realized in retrospect is that women naturally want to incorporate how to lead our sons and daughters as we strive to become leaders in political and business circles. And for making that a priority, I thank the women in business.

Therein lies an important key to how we will shift out of the patriarchal society

We must ensure our sons, in particular, are able to stay included and engaged, as today's young girls are demonstrating more ambition and fearlessness in their education and careers than boys are. Young women are filling up the seats in universities at a rate of 60 per cent and are, according to the professors I've interviewed, very self-directed. It is now the young men who are filled with testosterone and have no direction. We have two concurrent chapters going on in our lives as women. We have, on the one hand, our own glass ceilings and issues to deal with in attaining leadership roles. On the other hand, we currently have a generation of young men with no direction. Again, the mother, as the nucleus of the family, is in a position to develop strategies so that we ensure we direct ourselves and our young sons.

As I stood presenting to these women in business, I pulled out their local newspaper and pointed out how it revealed opportunities for advancing the community and themselves in business. I referred to two articles I had read in the local newspaper that day that summed up for me how they could make major strides toward developing the local economy while addressing social issues that concerned them.

The first one was a tiny article buried way in the back of the newspaper, which means it was of less importance to the editor than stories that are placed at the front of the newspaper. The article reported that the head of the local school board was raising some concerns about the lack of funding for the school district. He claimed that a drop in student enrollment would mean a loss of nearly $1 million in funding to the local schools, resulting in programs such as music, the arts, extracurricular activities, and breakfast and hot lunch programs for those in need, being cut. He went on to say that he was very hopeful that the stalled new housing developments at the local city hall would soon pass through so that the community could attract young families and tradesmen to town to increase enrollment, leading ultimately to an increase in funding and no program cuts.

Then I showed them the front page of the newspaper. On the cover there was a vocal special interest group opposing a new housing development in the community. This major development was one of several that had been stalled for as many as 10 to 15 years!

So I made the connection for them: "You are 90 women. There's your Manager of Economic Development, right here, happy to connect with you. He's been trying to get those housing developments passed at city hall and he needs *your* help so that in the end, the school district will get more funding in a more efficient manner to ensure the basic needs of children, seniors and the marginalized are not cut." I

challenged them: "Let's get down to city hall and *shape* that development to include low-income, family, and seniors housing."

There are methods for us to advance our community and connect
with our power in ways that may be new to us. When we have a funding shortage, we instinctively want to raise the money to fix it. And
with my background and passion for fundraising, I can tell you we
must continue to do these things. It is important for us to look deeper
and ask the proper questions about how to enhance the smooth running of our cities. The philosopher, Plato, likens the individual self to
the city. You will find more on this on the chapter on **Justice** through
a model of economic development that addresses our poverty issues.
The healthy running of a city can be likened to the healthy mind,
body, and spirit connection.

What if we wondered to ourselves whether there was a different way
to fix the challenges that underlie why we have one in five children
living below poverty? What if we asked the good questions of ourselves on how we can empower our communities and fix them?

Most of the women who attended the women's business function had
never been to city hall before and had no idea of their own power.
The next day I received a call from one of the women on the event
organizing committee and she said, "We're 90 women, we're going
down to city hall." And yet, in the same breath, she said, "I do hope
this Manager of Economic Development delivers for us." Well, in the
end, the power resides in you, the individual. We have to make that
last leap not to depend on the Manager of Economic Development
but to work with him/her to make the change and, if necessary, drive
the agenda ourselves—still counting on no one person, but working
together. That's the key and that's what the philosopher, Mary Wollstonecraft refers to at the beginning of this chapter on the importance
of virtues rendering us independent by ensuring we are guided by
our own reason. That is such an important revelation I am going to
say it again.

Virtues render us independent by ensuring we are guided by our own reason

At the end of my presentation to the women in business, instead of
asking me about business, I found the questions returned to the dis-

cussion of our children. This was really something I did not want to discuss, and yet these women showed *me* the importance of keeping our children top of mind. We must continue to lead upwards and back to our children.

One of the women in the audience asked me about the presentation I give to high school youth on visualizing their futures. I chose to gloss over it because I thought I was there to discuss business. The women taught me otherwise. And for that reason in part, I decided to write this book, to thank those women in business who taught me the very real importance of keeping our children the priority in everything we do in business and in politics. In fact, we have to. So my focus that day went from advancing myself professionally to advancing my children and me—*that* is what women are naturally good at. And that is what this book is about.

I wonder how we gain entry into the networks held by men if we are not provided with an introduction?

And I wonder if these networks are obvious—are they organized by name or are they organic and invisible webs of connected people?

Much of the entry into these male-dominated networks is based on language. Their members do not all necessarily demonstrate *The 7 Virtues*, but the solid leaders of ethics and character do, and those men are the ones we must look to for insights on how to connect to the networks where women need to be.

Those men who do not exemplify *The 7 Virtues* will NEVER be an entry point into the networks that you need to connect to. These men may appear to be connected, but trust me when I say they are not plugged into the power base that you want to connect with. The true power base that will advance you and your group consists exclusively of those people who exemplify *The 7 Virtues*. You will find them as a magnet attracts a magnet if you incorporate *The 7 Virtues* into your life.

The formula for success for women in leadership:

Phase 1: Build a solid foundation based on the daily practice of *The 7 Virtues.*

Phase 2: With the foundation of the Virtues, you are halfway to learning the current language of male-dominated networks in business and government.

Phase 3: Seek out individuals in business and government who exemplify *The 7 Virtues* and cultivate them as mentors who will help you learn the rest of the language.

Phase 4: Once you know the complete language, you can enter into the network or as the French philosopher, Jean-Jacques Rousseau called it, "The Social Contract." Then you will be a gateway for others. Although they may not speak the language, you can empower them to become a part of the social fabric of a healthy business and government life.

Consequently, the most perfect education, in my opinion, is such an exercise of the understanding as is best calculated to strengthen the body and form the heart. Or in other words, to enable the individual to attain such habits of virtue as will render it independent. In fact, it is a farce to call any being virtuous whose virtues do not result from the exercise of its own reason. This was Rousseau's opinion respecting men; I extend it to women.

– MARY WOLLSTONECRAFT

The philosopher, Mary Wollstonecraft, touched on all of these steps in her book, *A Vindication of the Rights of Woman.*

Independence through the virtues

The virtues are the foundation of independence. This is a crucial acknowledgement. For independence through the virtues will empower women no matter what their circumstances or conditions, to advance personally and professionally. It is worth noting that in focusing on "strengthening the body" (working out) and "forming the heart" (keeping our children top of mind), Wollstonecraft references another philosopher, Jean-Jacques Rousseau and his description of man with society. Wollstonecraft takes it further and says women deserve to live the virtues and reap the benefits of such philosophical living—not just men.

In his book, *The Social Contract,* published in 1762, Rousseau analyzed the relationship of man with society. He said that in the state of nature, man is in competition with his fellow men. Rousseau wrote of how man is more successful in facing threats by aligning himself and forming networks with other men. In this way, men connect with each other and form the combined grouping known as society. So in *The Social Contract* he wrote about the agreement that sets the conditions for membership in that society. And it was Mary Wollstonecraft who extended this same membership to women.

Wollstonecraft never intended for women to mimic men and go off and form groups for women only. What she intended was for women to network with men to advance society as a whole.

And yet in this modern age, when women have full membership in society, we realize that we still have far to go to obtain key positions. If you take Rousseau's social contract idea to a micro level, you can see that men form closed groups known to some as the "Old Boys' Clubs," as well as more formal networks such as boards, and chambers of commerce and government committees. It's crucial that today's women connect with these networks, with the goal of ensuring that all components of our society are served, and that means rich and poor, young and old, men and women of all races and cultures, and that everyone is at the table. One of the easiest and most powerful ways to connect with these networks is to sit on your civic committees.

Entry into the network—civic committees

Every year, your town, region or city advertises for volunteers to sit on civic committees. These groups deal with areas such as heritage, economic development, sports, gender issues, accessibility, plus there are unique committees that reflect what is happening in your own community. For example, the 2010 Olympic Games in British Columbia saw the creation of civic spirit committees whereby residents got engaged and had a say in how these monumental events impacted the community. ANYONE can sit on these committees. Members meet monthly and dialogue with Mayor, Council, staff and other residents. This is truly the most exciting way to connect to your community in a way that ultimately narrows the gap between rich and poor and ensures that women have a seat at the table. It is also crucial that you bring your unique perspective to the table to ensure the people you represent are heard.

It is not enough for a handful of experts to attempt the solution of a problem, to solve it and then to apply it. The restriction of knowledge to an elite group destroys the spirit of society and leads to its intellectual impoverishment.

- ALBERT EINSTEIN

Remember the rowing boat. When everyone is working in harmony towards a shared goal, there is order and success. You, therefore, have an obligation to get over any doubts or fears and begin to wonder what it would be like to stretch yourself and get engaged in your community committees—your first "what if" moment! And it costs nothing but your time. Come prepared with an open mind and get ready to grow and contribute in the most satisfying ways.

It is apparent from the numbers and stats there is a lack of women in leadership roles in business and government—that women have yet to obtain membership in society in the numbers that would reflect our equal representation.

If you break it down and follow the pattern above, you can see that we've essentially cracked the code on how to gain entry into the current patriarchal structure so that we can both advance ourselves, as women, and implement social reform through active and visible membership in policy-making groups that formerly did not include us.

Your network is your net worth

Hence, the importance of women building solid networks that include men. Women often join women's networking groups. These certainly can serve their purpose, but unless we build up the kinds of networks that Rousseau and Wollstonecraft describe, we will continue to repeat the cycle of staying on the outer fringes of politics and high-level jobs and this ultimately means that children will continue to live in poverty.

If the concerns of our society are not represented to the decision makers by the very people who are disenfranchised, then decisions cannot be made in balanced, healthy ways. Unless decision makers have some first-hand experience or understanding of the issues, they cannot pretend to understand. Decision makers count on hearing the voices of the people they serve.

Because most of the decision makers currently in business and government are white and male, they count on hearing the perspective of women in order to make the right decisions. While women's input is a positive step, we can do better by ensuring that more women of all cultural backgrounds are actively engaged in business and government at the decision-making level. Those women with first-hand experiences are better equipped to make decisions that will have positive and lasting impacts to reverse poverty, violence and accessibility issues.

Why would we join networks of women and not include the male networks that have already been established? Mary Wollstonecraft brings home the importance of ensuring women are provided with the same kind of education as men. This will empower us to attain the habits of virtue so that we may enter into the social contract and fabric of society. And here we are, over 200 years after the writing of her book and still many women are not aware of her teachings nor of the importance of Plato, Socrates, Rousseau and the great philosophers who shaped the language and state of today's worlds of business and government.

In labeling Wollstonecraft a feminist, when instead she should have been acknowledged as a great philosophical mind, we denied her work as a great philosopher. We denied many men access to her thinking and as a result, were unable to bridge some of our current gender gap because her writings were not exposed to men.

And now there are communities recognizing that everyone must have a seat at the table to ensure that we build healthy cities, towns and regions—using the works of the great philosophers as a foundation.

What *The 7 Virtues of a Philosopher Queen* sets out to do is create a road map for women to follow, based on what is good in the teachings of the great philosophers. It also offers an overview on why society is modeled in a patriarchal format and how a dramatic shift to a population of women will impact us in the future.

Reflect upon these statements:

• Sophisticated executives are self-directed.

• Companies need self-directed employees and aggressive leaders.

• Power supply comes from reaching one person at a time and deploying them.

Even I must admit that when I read these lines above, I nearly get scared out of my wits; at the same time, I have been known to be competitive and to live by and uphold these standards. Because if you recall, this is merely language set before us through a long-standing patriarchal model of business.

If you set about understanding these words as a language that represents skills and qualities you are more than capable of, then how would you feel? Would you judge these statements to be scary so quickly? When you read these lines, do doubts about your talents begin to set in? Again, it's merely the competitive language of the patriarchal society that might cause you to doubt your talents and abilities.

Let's set out to re-interpret what the statements are really asking of you and "decode" them.

Sophisticated Executives are self-directed.

Are you clear on your goals and what you know your mission is in your work? Do you have a personal mission statement?

Companies need self-directed employees and aggressive leaders.

Can you hold your own in ensuring your goals are reached? In the face of challenges, do you believe in your driving mandate enough to stand up for it regardless of what detractors say? Are you strong enough to ensure that you take nothing personally and persist in right action with the goal to getting your good work accomplished? Can you forget your ego and trust yourself to have the answers others need to hear?

Power supply comes from reaching one person at a time and deploying them.

Do you build relationships with the key people in your organization one-on-one to ensure that everyone feels ownership of the goals you have set out? Do you ensure that everyone feels that you are listening to them?

I was fortunate to meet incredibly philosophically-minded mentors throughout my life. As I reconnected with some of these mentors, it dawned on me that they had not only shaped me, but that they were mostly men. And my male mentors who influenced me for twenty years have a broad range of interests. They include a social worker, an army captain, a high-level political advisor, and a self-made millionaire. What they all shared with me was the belief that I could achieve my goals. And almost by osmosis, by being in their presence, I learned to speak their language.

So I have drafted my own 10 steps to speaking the language of the *New* "Old Boys." This plays off of the Old Boys' network to ensure we understand how they work and to ensure we are able to communicate with them.

10 Steps to speaking the language of the *New* Old Boys Network

1. Be intense. This is one of Brian Burke's 10 commandments in doing business. Brian Burke, the former CEO of the Vancouver Canucks, believes you need to be intense about your vision. He says, "Don't let anyone tell you you're too intense." While attending an economic development conference where he was speaking, I had the opportunity to thank Brian personally for giving me permission to be intense about my vision. I had never heard that this was not only acceptable but necessary. For years I would hear men say to me, "You're so intense." And I used to think that was a bad thing. No longer. Thank you, Brian Burke, for sharing this. For me, this was a "eureka" moment! I used to be so embarrassed for being intense. Now I walk with it, head high and chin up. I'm intense. And I'm me!

2. Get involved with government. Get to know the leaders from all levels of government in your community. Meet with them. Share your ideas with them. They will be able to assist you and your cause and will connect you with others. From Municipal Mayors and Council members to Provincial MLAs and Federal MPs, find out who they are. You can also invite them to speak at engagements or attend events to ensure they know who you are. Remember, they are just ordinary people and to serve the people is their job. And the ultimate result of true service is natural leadership. Quite possibly you may end up running for office yourself as a result. People that are already in government can connect you with people who can help you run for office. Volunteer and sit on the executive of a politician you believe exemplifies *The 7 Virtues*.

3. Golf. A great many relationships in business occur on the golf course, or at golf tournaments and particularly at golf tournaments at conferences. The generation of men from 35-60, more often than not, play golf. Younger business people may not be in the game yet. That's more than likely because they are starting out. Over time they, too, will see the benefits of networking on the golf course. Golf will also provide you with insights into the sportsmanship language of business and government. So if you have never played a sport and even if you have no depth perception like me, you want to get out golfing. It is also an incredible way to bond with your teenaged sons and daughters.

4. It's all in the delivery. I learned this in the 4-H Club in rural Nova Scotia as a child. Picture two cakes. One might be better made, but if it does not look better, it won't win the red ribbon at the 4-H county fair. In order to move forward, packaging yourself visually is part of the process in order to be heard. Wear power suits—nothing frilly. When in Rome do as the Romans do. The worlds of government and big business are owned by men. We have 82 per cent representation by men in government and over 90 per cent of the CEOs of large corporations are men. Therefore, you must fit into their world. People will make a decision about you in the first four seconds of meeting you. Ensure you are dressed in a well-fitted suit with simple jewelry, if at all. A classic watch, simple, well-polished shoes, and tidy, well-shaped hair. Straight hair is associated with being professional, while curly hair is perceived as wild and untamed. Women who straighten their hair are taken more seriously. I have naturally curly hair and you can bet I straighten it or wear it up on rainy days. I want to be taken seriously. I have a lot to say, and in order to help those living in the shadows not to judge me, I do these things.

What you wear affects 38 per cent of a person's view of you. There are people out there completely incapable of their work, but they are dressing the part and getting ahead. For that reason alone, recognize the importance of packaging your good work in a way that commands attention. There are people who need *you* to be a success, to achieve your mission. Make sure you package your soul so that it is heard.

I also find it interesting that the androgynous look is back. Tuxedo style shirts, tailored suit vests, pinstripes are all in style. These are classic pieces that allow you to look like the men in business and still feel feminine and stylish. I have filled my wardrobe with these pieces and I can see a difference when I emcee at an event or chair a meeting. The men fall in line and listen to me like a peer—they see me as no different—and my goal is to be taken seriously so I can deliver on the work I need to do.

5. Be a good sport. Know a few good jokes and be really happy and excited when you see your peers. You will never get away from chauvinistic comments, but you can learn to either laugh, or better yet, come up with a great comeback. I was golfing once at a tournament—there were two men and two women on our team. A very uncouth business man hollered across to the two men we were golfing with, "How'd you get the best looking girls on your team?" Now it's obvious that he thought this comment would flatter us and it's painfully obvious that he was oblivious to the feelings of the other women around us, so I hollered back, "I put the team together so I could get the best looking men on my team." I never heard another comment from him again.

6. Do what you can to assist other men and women to rise to the top. If you can be helpful by offering assistance, then you will receive assistance tenfold. Never, ever underestimate your ability to bring powerful men and women together or your ability to assist them. I recall when David Goldman from the Goldman clothier family wanted to meet with Chip Wilson of Lululemon. He asked me to arrange it and I did. We sat over coffee and talked fundraising and were able to connect their businesses. When asked by anyone in your path for assistance, help them. Continue to invest in other successful people and they will organically reciprocate should you need to call on them. Both of these titans in the clothier industry had been very good to me. So it is reciprocating those good acts back.

7. Make it look easy. Make work seem effortless. Don't complain about others or tell stories or talk of how busy you are. Don't complain that you have to do everything even if you do. Just keep your head high and do the work you need to do. People are smart, and they will take notice. Should you find some people unbearable or in the way, you can be sure that others feel the same way. But you don't need to tell them. Marcus Aurelius, the great philosopher whose mediations are read by the greatest presidents and leaders of all time, said that everyone was put on this earth for you to teach or to bear.

8. Learn about the infamous back door and learn how to access it. "Back door" and "front door" everything to ensure the objectives are met. Have high-powered connections that you can call upon to assist you with your objectives. When trying to pass something through, go the appropriate routes (the front door), but then call upon any connections you have (the back door) to put in a good word for you. When I applied for a program for my former city, I followed the proper protocol. I met with the bureaucrats, sent in the application and brought a letter from my Mayor. Then I contacted my local MP and asked him to do everything in his power to aid my non-profit cultural group. Having connections who could help me communicate how important this project was for the non-profits groups in order to make our community welcoming and more embracing of diversity and culture was crucial to the health of the community. I found champions in the community who could communicate how crucial this project was and they were able to support my project.

9. Get profile. Take any opportunity to speak in front of crowds or emcee events. This will position you in a place of authority. Get media interviews and articles written about you so that your name gets "brand" recognition. Ensure that you pour over every word and remember that each word you say on stage or in the media is precious—do not waste one word when you speak in front of an audience. People want to hear interesting stories that make you real to them. Be yourself. I started with a community radio show years ago. I took on every opportunity to emcee at my community radio station fundraisers. Then I moved into keynote speaking and have since been the emcee for major municipal functions, Rotary events and speaking at motivational events. I have been interviewed on CBC on many occasions and recently was a guest host on C100—the top ranking commercial radio station in my community. I began by volunteering to write a column years ago and now get paid to write a business column for The Chronicle Herald in my city of Halifax. You just start—volunteer and then it grows. I really enjoy meeting people who have read my column. I enjoy the fact that we have connected and they understand what I am here to achieve.

10. Build your niche. There is a mantra I have that literally flashes like a neon sign in my mind's eye—"work to your talents." Find out what you're really good at and make it your life's work. Just do what you are good at. Do what you were made to do. Follow your natural order. Become that expert in the thing you know best. What's amazing about doing this is that over time, it becomes effortless and you will not know the difference between work and pleasure as they will blur into one. You will be doing what you love all the time.

Now do your check-in and make the commitment to never doubt yourself again, and apply the virtue of wonder instead. This simple difference can set you on a brand new path, a path that was already laid out for you.

VIRTUE

II

Moderation

II

Having the fewest wants, I am nearest to the gods.

– SOCRATES

Freedom is not procured by a full enjoyment of what is desired, but by controlling the desire.

– EPICTETUS

Plato, the student of Socrates, who wrote *The Republic* believed that our biggest inner conflict arises out of our concerns for our own wealth and power. He believed that the goal of government and any system of laws must be to build a culture whereby people can be as happy and friendly as possible and *the good life* should not extend merely to the privileged elite.

Moderation

In many ways, understanding the virtue of moderation will bring you closer to true happiness. At first this statement may seem odd, but it's very true and can be proven through philosophical thinking.

The fact that the diet and credit card industries are booming in the billions of dollars is a major indication that we, as a society, have not mastered moderation. And oddly, in the pursuit of *perceived* happiness, we grow unhappier, heavier, and deeper in debt. North Americans spend billions of dollars on dieting and yet we've never been more overweight.

Our need for instant gratification in dieting—wanting a quick fix solution—is no different than our impulse to overeat. The two behaviours go hand-in-hand and we don't get the results we seek because we are not using moderation. Moderation is really delayed gratification, or simply just waiting longer before we reward ourselves with pleasures.

Another symptom is the rise in medication for Attention Deficit Disorder (ADD) for young children. We have placed our children in front of fast-moving images and given them fast food with no delayed gratification. No wonder they cannot control their impulses.

Knowing the difference between happiness and pleasure

The real hook in gaining perspective and a handle on moderation is first understanding the definition of happiness and the definition of pleasure and knowing the difference between the two. For it is the very confusion between the two that has caused our debt, weight issues and in some respects given rise to the increase in ADD.

When I talk to youth on visualization I tell them:

There are four things that can bring you happiness in life:

1. Love your work or studies.

2. A strong network of friends and family who support you and believe in you.

3. Volunteering. Volunteering is the fastest way to selflessness, which is when we are truly happy. In philosophy we must remove the ego in our learning if we are to become truly enlightened. Volunteering is the best way to forget about yourself and to genuinely think of others.

4. Take nothing personally. Forget your ego and focus upon the greater good. You will be able to move through challenging situations when you separate yourself from the work at hand. When we realize we are not so important we are able to really make change.

Now, what are pleasures such as dinner at a fine restaurant, clothes, cars and furniture? Don't they make us happy? The answer is no. Things cannot, in and of themselves, make us happy. However, we work hard and we deserve the benefits of enjoying pleasures. The key is not to mistake pleasures for happiness. A pleasure is a thing. So, for example, a new sofa cannot, nor will it ever, be able to bring you to a state of happiness. It is a thing. It may help you achieve a state of pleasure, but this will not be the lasting state of happiness. So if you know it brings you pleasure and you expect nothing more from it, then you will not be disappointed. It is only when we see or are convinced that these pleasures will make us happy, we begin the endless cycle of chasing the next fix by spending money, only to go further into debt in the incessant desire for happiness.

There is nothing wrong with having pleasures; however, it is crucial that you not confuse a pleasure with something that will make you happy. For a pleasure will never bring about true happiness.

Plato believed the ideal state is when we fulfill our true nature, and that *the good life* can only be obtained when we realize our truest capacities as human beings. He even went on to say that if you pursue pleasure in the belief that it will bring you happiness, it will surely destroy you.

Think again of the billion dollar diet industry and the fact that most North Americans are living with heavy credit card debt. Should you find yourself in either (or both) of these situations, take stock of Plato's philosophy and begin to really internalize the difference between happiness and pleasure. Then, set about applying this theory to your life to empower yourself to get on the track you belong. The answers are laid out within you, waiting for you to discover them.

> *If one oversteps the bounds of moderation, the greatest pleasures cease to please.*
>
> – EPICTETUS

Pleasure or happiness

Now that you see the difference between pleasure and happiness, you can control just about anything, from your eating to your spending habits. Do a check in on everything you do for a day and ask yourself, "Is this a pleasure, or something that can bring true happiness?"

And when examining the four things that bring happiness, ensure that you are giving them your fullest attention.

Each day, ask yourself the following:

1. Do I love my work or studies?

2. Do I surround myself with a strong network of friends and family who support me?

3. Am I volunteering and giving back to the community in a selfless way?

4. Am I able to let go and really invest and not worry about what people think about me?

I can guarantee you that if you spend your energies reflecting upon these four things, you will meet happiness and success like you had never imagined. In this chapter, you will read about a woman who went from being a high school dropout to a Ph.D. and then went on to launch a multi-million dollar fashion business. Use her story as an example for yourself of how each and every one of us has all the resources available to lead a life of true happiness.

If virtue promises happiness, prosperity and peace, then progress in virtue is progress in each of these for to whatever point the perfection of anything brings us, progress is always an approach toward it.

– PLATO

Tripartite Soul

Plato believed our soul has three parts that must live in harmony. And that our highest good is achieved only when these three elements are in balance and harmony.

Three parts of the Tripartite Soul are:

1. **Reason**–Powers of speech

2. **Spirited Element**–The ambitious, courageous, self-assertive and altruistic drives

3. **Bodily Appetites**–Pleasures

This ancient ideal really connects to the modern drive to have harmony among the mind, body and spirit. And again, this shows us that nothing changes over time. We, as humans, are the same as we were thousands of years ago, with the same desires, drives and challenges. They just manifest themselves differently today.

> *The just man (or woman) does not allow the several elements in his soul to usurp one another's functions.*
>
> – PLATO

It takes self-control and self-mastery to ensure that you keep all of the parts of your soul in harmony. That is why it is so important for us to have a true sense of self and self-awareness in order to authentically live a life of moderation and ultimate happiness.

Being programmed by a quick fix, ready-made solution offered by someone else is the last thing that will provide sustained balance, harmony, and joy in our lives. The three parts of the soul all have needs and must be satisfied, but only in harmony with *your* true nature. And only *you* can establish what that is through reflection and getting to know your inner self. "The Good Life" is truly the satisfying of the body, mind and spirit by fulfilling a life of virtue and excellence as a beautiful, healthy, strong and self-directed being.

We live in a culture of instant gratification. And when we are not in a strong state of self-awareness, we can succumb to the desires of the body for instant pleasure.

Because we are so used to getting everything quickly, compounded by the use of computers and television with fast visuals, we are finding it more difficult to wait. We want instant gratification. We want to get slim now. We want to get rich quick. We want to get a hit or high from food, images, or materialistic things immediately. But this instant gratification feeds our attention deficit as we never get long-term happiness and satisfaction from quick hits of gratification or pleasures.

The best thing we can do for our children is to delay gratification. We can teach ourselves to wait and savour pleasures; we do not need to have them right away. Once we can balance that with our other needs to learn and help others, then we begin to have more harmony and balance. You have to work towards it and ultimately you can experience it. It takes daily practice.

Top trends—life coaching and controlling our media

Plato's cave has become a metaphor for the way mass media influences every aspect of our current understanding of the events around us. It is no wonder Futurist Faith Popcorn predicted that the top trends for 2006 would be life coaching and controlling our media. These top trends of 2006 continue to be of significant importance for us today. Life Coaching is based on the philosophy that you already know what you need to lead a good life. The qualified life coach will help a person to uncover the answers they have within by using the Socratic method. Controlling our media means the pendulum is starting to swing back and we do not want to be bombarded by images. We want to control the messages and ideas that enter our lives. That is why Facebook, blogs and social media are popular. We want to control the messaging around us.

Household incomes double by removing the TV

I was told that removing the television from the living room doubles the household income. I know this to be true first hand. We cancelled our cable in 2001 and in the next five years, my income tripled. It's such a simple step and yet it can have such a big impact on your success and comfort level. When we sit for hours watching TV, those hours could have been used constructively to do many things from starting a business to studying, to connecting with our kids, to volunteering, to excercising, to reading a good book—to writing a good book—to do the things you want to do.

Turning off the barrage of outside messages allows you to sift through and find ideas that are more appropriate in supporting your life plan.

Now I am not saying no TV or news ever again; what I am saying is that you can control your media consumption. When I read the news it is online. I can click on the stories that are of interest to me and I am not waiting through broadcast stories that I do not find interesting or even worse, disturbing. And if there were a show that talked about Philosophical living and leadership, you can bet I would watch it.

Resources are your currency

Think of your resources as currency. If you invest all of your gifts and talents into your family and their concerns and nothing into your own personal dreams, then there will be no savings plan for you as your children grow. So if you were to take, say, ten per cent of your talents and time and invest them in yourself, whether by taking a course, volunteering, or starting a company, then you would have increased your personal net worth. By investing in yourself you can work towards ultimate independence while still supporting those around you. You do not have to give up one for the other. This is about achieving true personal and professional balance and harmony.

You have all the resources you need to lead a life of meaning

Lisa Palleson-Stallan is the owner of the yoga clothing company Lotus Wear. I met Lisa at a conference where I was speaking on economic development. Lisa approached me after the presentation and wanted to know how to get connected to the 2010 Olympic and Paralympic Games. Within two weeks of our meeting, I had the General Manager for the 2010 Commerce Centre at her store, and he was sharing with her how procurement works.

I have had Lisa speak at conferences since then, and what struck me about her is her gift of moderation. Lisa was a high school dropout who went on to earn her Ph.D. She became a business professor and then decided she wanted to be home with her three children. So she created her company. She has provided healthy competition in the yoga clothing market. What struck me beyond her courage was her ability to go without luxuries in the early days, to accomplish her vision. She took in home-stay students to help cover her mortgage, she packaged the clothing inventory in her basement, and she enlisted her husband, an accountant, to assist her with the mechanics of running the company.

When Lisa speaks to women in business, she strikes a chord every time. Her ability to go without and delay gratification to stay focused on her clear goal is an example of how to become successful and make your dream a reality. Nothing stopped Lisa from realizing her dreams.

Lisa is a real-life example of a woman who overcame the odds of going from high school dropout to the highest level of education, a Ph.D. And if that wasn't enough, she left a promising career to launch a multimillion dollar active-wear company because she wanted to spend more time with her children.

Lisa's choices were rooted in philosophical thinking. She followed her own authentic voice and refused to let others stop her from reaching her goals. As a student of contemporary philosophy, Lisa recognized that like anything, success is a process. And she realized that if she wanted a certain level of success, she needed a certain level of education. So she set about taking courses as a mature student at a community college.

Here is how Lisa describes her internal process toward making change. Notice that she balanced her own needs with those of the people she wished to serve, including her own family. This is the philosophical foundation of a meaningful, successful life.

Lisa's Story

"I think a lot of people doubt themselves and to be able to find what it is in life that works. It was a long journey, I went back to university and started taking basic courses and then I found that I was interested in political science and then moved into international development issues. And then I did my Ph.D. on intellectual property and empowering women. I ended up spending some time at a conference called 'The Conference for Biological Diversity' and I found that a lot of women had traditional knowledge and they weren't sure how valuable it was. So I then spent a couple of years researching women who had this traditional knowledge. And the biggest problem in the international trade system is that this knowledge is not recognized. And so I wrote my thesis on practical ways women could protect their knowledge such as how to use certain plants, certain remedies for medicinal purposes. Turmeric has a healing property and women from India would make into a paste and then large multinationals would put a patent on the paste and then these women were not able to use these age-old remedies without the threat of liability.

"It was a fascinating few years of conducting interviews at the WHO and seeing these paradigms. I had hoped to go on and teach this.

But there were so few jobs that I ended up teaching social marketing and then spent the next couple of years teaching at a university in Scotland. I enjoyed my job and I was excited about it and then I had my second son and found the pressures of trying to balance a career and having a child wasn't something that I was willing to do. I needed to find a work/life balance that would give me more control. And that is when we moved back to Vancouver. And then I found myself teaching part-time at Athabasca University and trying to figure out the next step.

"And that got me to thinking about starting Lotuswear.

"When I was younger, any kind of change used to frighten me—I think that you get so used to making choices out of what society expects and I think that eventually you take your first risk and then after that the risks are less tough to take. And even if you fail, you ultimately learn to keep going."

Lisa's lesson

Lisa recognized that listening to your authentic voice, what you know to be true, and then following through on that regardless of the outcome, will take you to a life of meaning and success.

Reflections on moderation in starting a business

Lisa's journey reveals that the path to success is not clear cut, but if you trust your instincts and follow the things that truly bring you happiness you will achieve your vision. And moderation is a virtue that helped Lisa progress from high school dropout to self-made business woman.

"The biggest thing for me is that once I decided to give up my teaching career, I always thought that I had worked so hard for this job. Once I had my kids, I began to question if this is the thing that I wanted to do. Giving up this career, we went from double income to one income. At that time I did not realize how long and how hard it would be to get the business where it is now.

"We scaled back from two cars to one car. We had enough money so we could buy a house but in order for me not to work, we took in home-stay students. You go from not having to worry about watching your money to now having to watch every penny. We had a couple of holidays a year that we had to give up. We had the luxuries that now we could not afford because we were putting our own money into the business. It is different when you have an investor. But when it's your money, you have to be careful. There is nothing to spring back from. If the money runs out, that is it.

"I think that the most important thing is that *moderation bounces off of balance.* To a certain degree you have to put in an excessive amount of time. Your business is an extension of your relationship. We feel so lucky that we have built something together. Andrew (my husband) and I spend more time together now because we are fortunate to work together. It has made our relationship stronger—now we have a common goal. And yet, we pour everything into the family.

"We have been able to live a much more balanced life. Our family is more important. You do not have to compromise your values or what you believe in to meet success. I have had to detach myself emotionally from the business in some ways because you do not want to wear that home."

Your creativity is a resource

Lisa continues with the point that your own creativity, rooted in the virtue of wonder, is a powerful resource. And that the creative mind, the mind that wonders rather than doubts, allows people to work more effectively and deliver better results.

"Most businesses fail in the first year—80 per cent fail. And often it is because the owners become so entrenched in the business, and they refuse to let go. They refuse to give anyone ownership. They refuse to empower others in the business to take ownership. Change happens every season in the fashion industry. You must let go and adapt and allow people you trust to be autonomous.

"That is how we went from a one store company to a seven-store company in two years. We invited others to believe in the philosophy of Lotuswear. The people built the culture of Lotuswear.

"Lotuswear's philosophy is to empower people to work in the city that they love and to really work in an area that they feel good about. We allow people to work to their talents and to be authentic and to feel ownership. When you have people who love what they do, they work differently."

Lisa's message to other women

"I think that so many of us ignore our potential for success for too long. I encourage every woman to do whatever it takes to facilitate making decisions at the crossroad and to take that step. And even if you take that step and you fail, you will still be better off than if you had never taken that step at all.

"I have taken that step and I have failed but it gives you the confidence to take that step again until you meet success. I think in that first step you actually do it and you find it's not as scary as you thought it would be. But what if you stay where you are and do not take a risk? That is even scarier. I knew that if I didn't take the step I would have stayed exactly where I was. It is so much easier to be comfortable where you are, but it is so much more satisfying and life-giving to stretch."

Courage to start a business—self-awareness is the key

Starting a business takes the ability to assess and take on risk. And yet, it really does return to how well you know yourself. Connecting with your authentic self is crucial to success in business as Lisa demonstrated in her story.

To thine ownself be true.

– SHAKESPEARE

Acclimatize Communications Corp

Lisa's story reminds me of when I started my company, Acclimatize Communications Corp. in 2001. In the second year of my business, I was interviewed for a paper on "An Entrepreneurial Perspective of Risk Taking, Leadership and Learning" at Simon Fraser University.

I thought the writer best summed up what drove me to start my company when she quoted me in the closing element for the paper. I include that excerpt here for anyone considering going into business (and I say if you have done your homework, go for it!!!)

"I think that leaders are people who are really listening to whatever you want to call it, their inner voice or their soul or their subconscious, whatever, it's all the same. But if you truly listen to that, then you will become a leader because you will go off the beaten path and go do what it is that you're meant to do. I think that's a problem for a lot of people who are unhappy in their lives and go plugging away working for someone; they know they're supposed to be doing something else but they don't know how to get there. And so the leader is the person who says, 'Well, I don't fully know how to get there, but I'm going to figure out how to do it,' and they go off and do all the learning and the risk taking to get there. I think that most people are capable, especially the few who are willing to listen to themselves and go and do it."

When you go into business, you learn so much about yourself. You are the one making the decisions. Because you must hold yourself accountable for the results, you become more accountable than you ever dreamed possible. Being accountable is an attribute that will carry you to success. And being accountable crosses over into all aspects of your life, from professional to personal, and how you treat the health of your mind, spirit and body.

Healthy Diet

Thou shouldst eat to live; not live to eat.

– SOCRATES

• Estimated number of adults around the world who are overweight: One billion

• Percentage of Canadians who say they are overweight or obese: 38

• Percentage who are overweight or obese according to their BMI (Body Mass Index): 49

• Estimated number of obese two to 17 year olds in Canada: 500,000–Proportion of Canadian children who are overweight or obese: Nearly one in three—Percentage of obese children at three years of age who remain obese into adulthood: 30

• Average number of hours per week two-year-olds watch TV: 14—Percentage of all meals the average family consumes while the TV is on: 60—Percentage of kids under six who have a television in their bedroom: 36

• Estimated number of commercials children view each year: 20,000–40,000—Rank of food among most frequently advertised product category on U.S. children's TV shows: One

• Number of Canadians who say their diet is very healthy: One in three

• Single serving size of Coca-Cola sold in 1950s: 6.5 oz—Single serving size now: 20 oz

• Percentage of overweight adolescent girls who report being teased about their weight: 96—Percentage of high school teachers who strongly agree "most people feel uncomfortable when they associate with obese people": 43

It is better to rise from life as from a banquet—neither thirsty nor drunken

– ARISTOTLE

I have a Body Mass Index (BMI) of 22. This means I am in the normal range of weight. Now, the ideal BMI is between 18.5 and 25, which means I am in the middle part of the healthy range. And yet, I cannot tell you how many people call me slim!!! I am not slim—I am in the middle range of normal. Normal. Not slim.

I recall being at a Christmas party and getting my plate of food and someone saying, "How do you stay so slim?" This same person then returned for a second plate of food. Now, before you go thinking, "How dare she think it's so easy?" believe me, I *do* know how challenging weight can be. I was 210 lbs at the age of 15. I could not walk past a school bus without being called every name imaginable. I was overweight for my entire childhood, from age 5–15.

How did I lose the weight and keep it off? My parents separated. All the stress was over and I could get on with living. Has it been easy? Absolutely not. Once you have used food as your vice, keeping the weight off is a daily exercise. What was interesting in my journey though was that a friend told me I was smart, but that no one at high school was going to want to get to know me because of the excess weight. I found that to be a real shame, since I thought I had some interesting things to say. Imagine if I had let weight keep me from connecting with people. So I got rid of it. I got rid of anything that was going to keep me from communicating the things I felt were important.

I had the extra weight because I was upset about my parents. Once the stressful marriage ended, I was free to remove the visible marker (weight) from my life.

How did I set about losing the weight? I got rid of anything that caused me to overeat. The stresses were gone from my parents' strained marriage. I refused to spend time with anyone who over-ate, for I did not have the will-power to stop myself if they were overeating. That meant an overhaul of the people I spent time with. I was able to keep people in my life if they were able to join me in the power walks and diet. Every cousin and friend of mine was on a diet that summer! We power walked, dined on air popped popcorn on Friday nights with movies, and talked a lot about the future.

These walks/talks were very invigorating and we began to discuss things that we would never have discussed while previously overeating in front of our televisions.

Overeating has become more acceptable to the general population

Where is your critical thinking as an individual?

What I really find interesting about all of this is that on the one hand, it is our culture that accepts overeating to be OK. And on the other hand, there is still pressure by the media for people to be super slim like the Hollywood images. We are so influenced by the images and media and people around us that if you look at the obesity stats above, it's almost become acceptable to be overweight in our everyday lives and concurrently, to be in a constant state of stress by wanting to be an unattainable ideal. So we end up doing nothing about either the weight or the stress of wanting to be slim.

Now here's where philosophy comes into place. We need not care whether it's acceptable or not by society's standards to be overweight. Nor should we be trying to become unattainably skinny like the Hollywood images. For the philosopher is not controlled or dictated to by others' ideas of what is right and wrong. If you treat your body as a vessel with which you carry your soul and intellect, then treat your body with respect, but do not give it too much attention.

So this means you would do all the things to ensure it is functioning properly—that you exercise, eat moderately and think nothing more of it. Then give it no further attention. For your body is material. If you recall Plato's allegory of the cave, the body is the cave, and you must get beyond it to see the light. In other words, your higher purpose is where your energies should be spent. Your energy should be spent on your intellect and reasoning, which transcend the body.

What was empowering about my desire to lose weight when I was young were my reasons for losing it. I was so scared that no one would want to get to know my soul because of the weight, and I believed so strongly that I had things to do and say—so I set about freeing myself from it.

Your body as your work of art

I also visualized what my body would look like. I saw my body clearly as a sculpture already inside the clay. I saw the weight as being no part of my inner being and knew that by removing the outer layer of fat, the "clay" that the work of art, the sculpture, would emerge. And it did.

I thought it was very funny when I returned to high school after the summer, having lost 60 pounds in the previous six months. No one recognized me. It was as if I was a new person. Of course, I carried the mindset of an overweight person around with me at first. And then I got over it. I embraced the sculpted work of art that I had un-covered beneath the clay.

Now, like anyone who has dealt with their weight, I have yo-yoed over the years. What I have found interesting yet somewhat sad is that every time I gained even 15 lbs, I was treated differently. Now, I am not sure if this has to do with the loss of confidence in myself or just the way I looked. And it doesn't really matter. What matters is that obviously I was not taking care of myself for some reason, and it showed. The lesson: people will not necessarily want to treat you with respect if you're not treating yourself with respect.

As I re-read the stats on weight and obesity above, I noticed that TV has a great deal to do with our weight issues. And I find it interesting that the most stable my weight has been, with no fluctuations either way, occurred within the time frame since I cancelled our cable.

Our outer bodies can reveal our inner state. People were uncomfort-able with my extreme weight because I was saying to the world, "I'm not comfortable."

And if everything in life is measurable, as in science, you can conquer weight on your own. If you allow someone to tell you what to eat at what time of the day, you will never know what your own body needs.

It is simple science. Eat less, exercise more. Eat 1,300–1,500 good cal-ories a day when you want, when you feel like it. Make them veggies, fruit, complex carbs and lean protein. That's all you need to do. Your body does not need more than this if you are trying to lose weight.

Add some exercise: 45 to 60 minutes every day, and voila! You will be the perfect work of art that you dared dream of. Remove everything that keeps you from reaching your personal goals from your life. And if you love your friends and family and they are keeping you from getting there, enlist them in your walks and talks and share with them your new life plan. Stay away from anyone that does not want to do this with you until you're stronger and can find the strength to be around them and influence them. Only you will know what you are capable of doing and what works best for you.

What is interesting is how much attention we give to our weight. Imagine spending all of your days thinking about your body weight, doing nothing about it, and then wondering where your life went.

Life is a test

I believe life is a test. There is temptation all around us. Focus on what you need to do to accomplish the work you were put on this earth to do, and attend to it. Trust that you have the answers already and set about self-discovering them. You know what feels right to you. Trust that part of your instinct.

Moderation in our work

Alexander the Platonist cautioned me against frequent use of the words, "I am too busy" in speech or correspondence, except in cases of real necessity.

– MARCUS AURELIUS

There also seems to be an imbalance in our work lives. I often see people running so fast, often looking disheveled or flustered because they have taken on too much. And then when you ask some of these people how they are, they say, "Oh busy, overworked, so much going on."

We have bought into a culture that tells us to be busy bees, and if you circulate with A-type personalities then you know there is a certain expectation that you will take on a great deal of work. I have also seen that as women, we will take on work loads for others and compensate for their inability to do their jobs because we somehow bought into the idea as a nurturer that we have to take care of everyone, even at our own expense.

Whether it's an issue of just getting the work done or there is a certain need to be seen as valuable, it is important to examine your response to the demands of others. Know your limits and be clear when you believe a project or job is not something you can execute with your current work load. Or find the resources you need and demand the tools you need to execute your work. One of the biggest challenges of any business is to empower staff with the tools they need to do their jobs effectively. By compensating and not demanding the resources you need, only *you* will suffer.

Think of Lisa's style of leadership at Lotuswear. She trusts her team to do what they need to do to deliver the results and to follow through on their mission. Whether you are in management or not, you must have the tools you need to deliver on your job. Focus on wonder, apply moderation, and be resourceful in delivering the results you want.

Also, ensure you are paid what you are worth. I spoke with a male consultant as I was establishing my fees for my company and realized it was time for me to bump up what I ask for. We were discussing this and he said that many of the men in his private club circles complain about these *younger* women who will work for less. So know your worth. If you know your value in the workplace or in your business, then demand it. Find some peers (a mix of men and women), and talk with them one-on-one to find out what the industry standards are for your work. For if you are getting paid what you are worth, then you will not need to take on so many projects and you will be able to maintain balance in your life.

A Philosopher Queen is rational under any circumstances

Ensure that your work pace, exercise, responsibility, learning, friends and family are in harmony so that you can be rational under any circumstances and make the wise decisions needed to move you and your projects and personal life forward.

Take stock of your life and where you invest your time and how satisfying this is for you.

There is moderation even in excess.

– BENJAMIN DISRAELI

III

Truth

III

Truth has no special time of its own. Its hour is now—always and indeed then most truly when it seems unsuitable to actual circumstances.

- ALBERT SCHWEITZER

A lie can travel halfway around the world while the truth is just getting out of bed.

- MARK TWAIN

The Triple Filter Test

You may have read the "Triple Filter Test" by Socrates; it's a story that I have seen circulated by email in the past. It truly stands the test of time and demonstrates why integrating philosophy into our everyday lives can have significant positive outputs. Keep this philosophy in mind the next time you either hear, or are about to be tempted to repeat, a rumour or gossip.

In ancient Greece (469–399 BC), Socrates was widely lauded for his wisdom. One day the great philosopher came upon an acquaintance who ran up to him excitedly and said, "Socrates, do you know what I just heard about one of your students?"

"Wait a moment," Socrates replied. "Before you tell me I'd like you to pass a little test. It's call the Triple Filter Test." "Triple filter?" "That's right." Socrates continued. "Before you talk to me about my student, let's take a moment to filter what you're going to say." "The first filter is Truth. Have you made absolutely sure that what you are about to tell me is true?" "No," the man said, "actually I just heard about it and…" "All right," said Socrates. "So you don't really know if it's true or not." "Now let's try the second filter, the filter of Goodness. Is what you are about to tell me about my student something good?" "No, on the contrary…" "So," Socrates continued, "you want to tell me something bad about him, even though you're not certain it's true?" The man shrugged, a little embarrassed. Socrates continued, "You may still pass the test though, because there is a third filter—the filter of Usefulness. Is what you want to tell me about my student going to be useful to me?" "No, not really."

"Well," concluded Socrates, "if what you want to tell me is neither True nor Good nor even Useful, why tell it to me at all?"

This modern-day translation of the great ancient philosopher Socrates is so easy to apply to our lives. And that's what we are setting out to do—to apply these ancient ideals in real, applicable ways so that we may lead authentic, meaningful lives.

In the days before his death, Socrates was focused on one question: *how to be excellent at being human.*

The surest way to be excellent at being human is to follow the virtues

The Socratic Method has been likened to an art sculpture. Just as the artist chips away at layers of the clay to get to the art work within, the Socratic Method is used to strip away all suppositions that are in opposition to what is true about any given thought or idea. So in a sense, it focuses on the negative so that it can be removed to reveal the positive—the truth.

Life Coaches and instructors who use the Socratic Method do not tell others what they should do; instead, they employ questions as a way of testing the things that he or she is teaching or encouraging.

So in order for you to engage in the Socratic Method, you must think, reflect, and use critical thought to chip away and find your truths. Then you apply these truths to your life and incorporate them into your belief system so that you move to a level whereby you can see the truth in any given situation and take right action regardless of the situational challenges.

The Socratic Method requires that you follow the rules of logic. This means you choose reason over the senses. The coach or teacher's line of questioning is mapped out to reveal to the student or client where her reason is flawed. When you develop your abilities to think logically and to use rational thought in all situations, you get the desired effect of right action and proper decision making.

Socrates believed that our answers are innate within us and that we can bring this knowledge of the truth forward through questioning.

There are certain basic truths that we learn and then implement in our lives later on. The following is the story of my chance encounter with author and artist, Ben Wicks, and how he challenged me to see my role as a parent in a new light. I learned some crucial truths about parenting from Ben Wicks that would serve me as a parent greatly years later. I wish to share this life-altering experience with you, for it truly can help us lead our children with conviction and direction during the often challenging times of parenting. This is important particularly for our young boys as we shift out of the patriarchal society.

You are your child's first teacher–a meeting with Ben Wicks

When my son was just 16 months old, I joined the legions of harried housewives down at the Sears bargain basement. I was there, like everyone else, to find the deals you brag about to your mother-in-law. I was on high shopping alert that particular day, on the lookout for clothes for my pabulum-consuming first child who seemed to pop the snaps on his body-suit undershirts faster than I could change his cloth diapers. Yes cloth, not out of some environmentally conscious choice solely, but also out of forced budgeted survival. Little did I know that I would leave the department store that day with a deal that would change my entire outlook on parenting and my role in the only job that doesn't come with a job description and has no standard operating procedures manual.

That day, the famed cartoonist, Ben Wicks, was visiting our town as part of his book signing tour. My 16 month-old son was well rested and most agreeable, so we bought the paperback called "Born to Read" for $2 and I was able to read a good part of it while waiting in line to meet Ben Wicks. I read two things in that lineup that changed my direction as a parent:

1. There's one thing more important than reading to your child—your child needs to see you reading something you enjoy first.

2. *You* are your child's first teacher.

When our turn came, it seemed as if there was no one but my son and Ben Wicks in that crowded bargain basement. At that time I was 27, and I recall that the only thing my single friends could offer me were the cutest baby outfits and advice on how I should get out more often. No fault of their own—they had no kids. Naturally, my maternal mind and instincts were so ready for the conversation that would ensue that I can still, to this day, return to our conversation and feel Mr. Wicks' complete attention on my son and me and our discussion at the Sears bargain basement.

When I got to Ben Wicks, I wasn't hurried along as I thought I would be, but rather, invited to discuss the book. I had never before been told that I was my child's first teacher. This was a brand-new concept to me and one that I found very appealing. Mr. Wicks' warm smile and attentiveness revealed his delight that his words were precious insights for me, and he could tell that I was excited to finally have some direction in this wonderful yet sometimes painful journey of parenting.

I recall being so curious about how much more important it is that I be observed reading by my child. We had always been told how vital it is to read to your child and how we should read to them in the womb and play classical music to them.

But no one had explained that my child should see *me* reading, and often. Wow, it was as if a light came on. And then it becomes so much greater. The concept of reading books that I like is not only about being a real life example, but by osmosis, they know that we, as parents, enjoy this—that reading is not homework, not something we have to do, but rather an enjoyable experience. So if my child sees how I enjoy reading on my own, then he'll want to too. It's really so simple. Somewhere in there, as if it were his real intention in the first place, Mr. Wicks has shown us how important it is to take time for ourselves as parents, and that maybe it's time to really show our children that parents, through the example of reading, need to take time for ourselves in order to be recharged and ultimately be fully available as parents when we need to be.

This whole notion that you are your child's first teacher is such an empowering concept. And Mr. Wicks didn't mean just the support you provide before Miss Jones, the kind kindergarten teacher, enters your lives. He meant the whole trip right until the end of secondary school. You become the all-important teacher support staff who ensures that your child is getting a complete education.

This made me realize why parents get broken up when their child leaves the nest and why some parents have been known to get weepy when they drop their kids off at college. This is when parents realize that they are no longer their child's first teacher, that the world is now their teacher, and time's up—they've had their chance.

> **You have one shot at giving your children a magical childhood and then time's up—you've had your chance.**

I made a deal with myself then and there in the middle of the Sears bargain basement that I would read every chance I could get and that I would support my son (and eventually a daughter, too) and their teachers with whatever challenges we would face.

And we've had a few challenges.

I learned an important skill at the age of 25. If you don't like the way things are going, zap yourself in time in your mind to the age of 80, examine your regrets fully and then return to the age you are now.

Now make the changes while you still can

It is vital that when you sense that things aren't going smoothly you see how terribly out of control they can become. Not a pleasant experience, I realize, but a lot easier to deal with in imaginary land before it becomes your reality. This is the fastest way to get the courage to create honest dialogue and make change now. You'll be surprised at how wonderful people can be when you raise your concerns and offer suggestions for change.

When my son was six weeks into grade one, I had this gnawing feeling that his teacher wasn't the best fit. It might have had something to do with the fact that she couldn't add simple numbers. At first I thought the slip-up on the first day of school was due to nerves with all the parents around, so I let it go and chuckled with her and everyone else supportively as she corrected herself.

The discomfort grew over the weeks, as I would make visits with a forgotten lunch or to pick my son up for an appointment, only to discover the children scattered about the classroom with no order. One particular day I dropped in to find my son trying to print in his journal, but walking around not knowing how to get about the business of printing. His two little friends were staring into space and there was no stimulation or order in the room. Later that evening, I asked him about his new class and learned that most of the days were spent running around in the gym. He went on to say that it felt like they played too much.

Then, at parent-teacher night, I noticed a few things that just didn't sit right. It wasn't so much the fact that she told each parent the same cookie-cutter analysis of their child's work and progress, but what she told one particular family. I recall feeling somewhat saddened for this particular child whose parents blew in only to talk with the teacher, having opted out of the child-led tour of their new class and school displays. I couldn't help but overhear the conversation. The teacher was telling these parents that it was perfectly normal that their six-year-old child didn't know his alphabet yet. Pardon?

I decided I would give it one last shot, that another impromptu visit during class time would show me that it was all in my head that I was an overprotective, self-employed suburban housewife with way too much time on her hands. I told myself I was being silly, it was just bad timing and she was a teacher who deserved a chance to reveal how wonderful she is. Walking in to discover this teacher yelling at a child to the embarrassment of the janitor knocking on the door was it for me.

I immediately drove to the neighbouring school, dried my eyes, tried to remain composed and asked to transfer my son. I was told that we had to live in the district, and there was one spot left. I asked her to hold it for me as my son would be joining them before month's end.

The next day the realtor took us out to the desired school district's neighborhood and we submitted a bid on a house.

The toughest part of all this was returning to speak with the wonderful principal at my son's former school. She was so kind, so patient with my concerns that I began to wonder if I had made a mistake. And then I realized, in one sentence she said, I had been right. In that one sentence, I learned to stick with my convictions and to hold fast to the fact that I am my child's first teacher. The very patient and progressive principal told me, "There will be teachers who you won't approve of throughout your child's education and you can't keep moving every time this occurs."

You see, this is where she was wrong.

This is where I had a very philosophical moment and quietly said inside, "Just watch me." You see, you *can* change things that aren't working. I realized that I have a very small window of opportunity to direct my child and to be my child's first teacher. And yes, I will pack up and move, every time my son is left in the charge of a complacent teacher. Just as I know I won't hesitate to pack up and move if he someday runs with a rough crowd. I will have plenty of time to relax during my retirement, so I don't mind a bit of movement now for peace of mind later.

Philosophical parenting—with direction and purpose

Now to qualify this to the outside world: sure I may appear overprotective, and that's fine too. I really don't spend too much time concerning myself with what others think about my behaviour. In fact, in this busy world, most people aren't concerned at all about what you're doing; they're busy trying to make decisions they can feel good about for their own families.

Remember, the principal's own interests were clearly different from mine. She did not want to rock the boat and feared that a parent's moving because of a teacher's inability to teach could send terrible messages and weaken morale. So I did the right thing for my family and did nothing to harm the school or the experience of others. Far be it from me to tell others what they need. I trusted what we needed and set about ensuring I was fulfilling my job as my child's first teacher.

Bearing this in mind, I didn't feel it necessary to chat about the move at all. When we moved to another school, I certainly didn't make a deal of it. I didn't bring it to anyone else's attention, no rallies, no complaints filed–I just quietly transformed my child's world into a place of comfort for our family. Besides, we had a great excuse to leave the school–we were moving to a new house.

Ben Wicks–creating our own "unique life pictures"

I often think about the show Ben Wicks had on television when I was a child. I recall watching him create a visual out of thin air. In seconds, he would sketch something so absolutely wonderful with his black felt marker. I remember trying to watch his hand movements to see if I could find out *how* he created his masterpieces. He always created so swiftly, so gracefully with such ease of the pen. He knew what he was mapping out. He visualized it and made it happen without hesitation.

Just like his drawings, I learned that we have to visualize what we want to create and make our individual visions happen. We have just a moment in time to make our mark through visualizing good things, no matter how much work it requires. We can trust our own creativity and knowledge to make the next move in creating our own unique life pictures.

Truth–you are your child's first teacher!

Say this one out loud and say it to as many people as you can: "I am my child's first teacher." This was Ben Wick's message, and we can all help his insights live on by saying it and living it. This makes us accountable as parents.

I recall sharing this insight one day with a neighbour who was complaining that her son's tutor cost so much and that it was hard on her son. I shared with her the Ben Wicks story and how reading should not be associated only with the tutor and not being able to go out and play every day after school. Her son should associate reading with fun. And when I shared with her that we are our children's first teachers she said, "No I am not." This mother firmly believed that her child's kindergarten teacher was her son's first teacher.

This is such a dilemma for modern society. It was only in the past century that school systems as we know them were created. Up until the past 100 years, parents were the child's first teachers. It has been this way throughout time.

As we shift out of the patriarchal society, remember it is our sons that we need to be mindful of in ensuring that they are feeling a sense of purpose and direction. We are seeing more self-directed young women and many lost young men who say to themselves, "Do I want to be a rap star or should I join a terrorist group?" This is happening to some youth today. This is our reality. Youth violence is steadily on the rise in North America.

The best thing you can do is cancel your cable, head to the library and get library cards for your entire family. Sit by the fire and crack your favourite book. If your budget permits, head on over to Chapters and let your family go wild and have a seat in Starbucks and read that book.

We have library cards and now that we are doing better financially, bookstores have become some of our favourite places. The magic of words and pictures can transport you to far-away lands, distant times, and most of all, teach you something you did not know before. Books create opportunities for parents and children to share interests and to talk to each other. We learn more about ourselves and learn so much more while engaged in a good book than sitting in front of the TV.

Your child is less likely to be confused by the clutter of TV ads and competing images for his or her attention if reading is a focus and seen as a delight in the home. There is something calming about a home with music and books. Remember, household incomes increase by 50% on average when there is no TV in the living room, so there are added incentives.

We cancelled our cable the week of 9/11. I, being a journalist and news junkie, could not tear myself away from the news. But for my own peace of mind, I cancelled the cable that week so that we could have calm in our home. Now, I still get the news online and visit Canada.com every day to find out what is happening. But I can click the stories I want to read. I do not have to sit and wait for a story that I find disturbing or let myself be inundated by ads that are mindless while I wait for the news that matters to me.

Control your media

This is very, very important to the success in your life: control your media. Eighty per cent of our thoughts can be negative. This can be attributed to the negative images and messages from media and advertising all around us. If you can control your media, you will be able to think more clearly, be more focused, and you will become far more self-directed.

So I choose to read *Oprah Magazine* when I am relaxing. I choose to visit Canada.com for my news. I choose to rent documentaries that I want to watch. I choose to read books on Churchill, Plato, Socrates, Mary Wollstonecraft, Simone de Beauvoir and other great thought leaders.

In 2005 I chose to write my own newspaper column and called it "The Good Life." The column came out every two weeks in our local NOW newspaper in Coquitlam, BC, and I wrote it for two years until I moved back home to Nova Scotia. In the column I wrote about how three levels of government, non-profit and private sector, work together to build a healthy community. It was a social column with a focus on the star power of non-profit organizations. These organizations were always doing something fantastic around resolving some kind of challenge. I think non-profit organizations are true heroes, and I applauded them in every single column by placing them with other local business "celebrities" and political leaders. I wrote "The Good Life" for free. That is how important the message was to me and I learned from so many people in the community that it was a big part of bringing them together. City hall staff used to tell me that if they wanted to really know what was going on in their community all they had to do was read my column.

When I returned to Nova Scotia, I began writing a similar column, "Culture Shift," for the province's major daily newspaper, The Chronicle Herald. I still write this column and it appears in the business section. I really feel there is an important place in the world of business for philosophical thinking that ensures no one is left behind and this means fostering a sense of how non-profit, government and business need to understand each others' goals and needs—and it begins by seeing our role in each others' lives.

I do love writing this column and I am always moved when a typed letter arrives for me, and when I get an email or a phone call. When people take such time to say, "Your column put into words what I have always felt." For me that is when I know I have come closer to achieving my life's work. I know that I am on this earth to help bring context around the events in our lives to real people. I am here to push for change and to take people out of their comfort zones through the virtues. And every day I seek out positive opportunities to do this.

Working for yourself

Part of the reason I became self-employed was that while I was working under someone else's schedule, I found myself losing touch with important things because of my family's hectic lifestyle. On one occasion I couldn't find my son's report card because it had fallen between the cracks of the table. And it felt as if our grip on his schooling and life in general, was slipping too.

Self-employment gave me control of my hours and our lives in so many ways. And it gave me the freedom and time to volunteer and write my column.

What would you be doing right now if you knew you could not fail?

Years before I started my company, when I was writing for a local TV show, a producer took a pewter sign with the above quote written on it and placed it on the edge of my cubicle. And she said to me, "What would you be doing right now if you knew you could not fail?"

Ask yourself this question

When I did, I was amazed at what came out of my mouth. I said, "I would be running my own company." And that's exactly what I did. There is a certain comfort in stripping away all the fears and societal messages that make us think we can't do certain things. Having been raised with very little, I always thought operating a company was for the wealthy. Then I realized, by questioning and observing myself, I had demonstrated to myself and to others that I could do this. Since I had the proven capacity to guide companies in strategy, there was no reason that I couldn't do this for myself as well.

In order to find your own truths, you must ask yourself these types of questions.

Take a note paper and pen and begin the daily practice of self-examination. Here are two important questions to start with:

1. What would you be doing right now if you knew you could not fail?

2. On what do you base your decisions? Facts, experiences, the opinions of others? To ensure you're connecting with your own experience—your own truth—rather than the opinions of others, write down your source of information and how that source earned your trust. In this way, when you make a decision it is really yours.

Beliefs are the rules of your life. If you believe something to be true, then it is. By questioning your life rules using the above two questions, you will be able to ensure that your belief system is a positive one. You want to ensure your own truths are ones that will carry you to your goals.

You *can* choose your beliefs. If you do not like the results you are getting, you can use self-examination to outgrow beliefs that do not serve you in reaching your goals.

Every one of us has access to the resources to reach our goals and shape our beliefs through true experience. This means we need to take action to validate our self-confidence by showing ourselves what we are capable of. Your inner resources are waiting to be tapped into. You can discover your inner wisdom by self-questioning and then taking action. The action part is just as important as asking yourself the important questions.

Recognize setbacks as gifts

It's amazing to hear someone say that they can't do something, or that it's not in their nature to do something. I think this is the most tragic myth on earth and it saddens me to witness anyone making such statements. My former husband used to say that he was shy and nervous because his mother was like that and, therefore it's in his nature. And yet, when in the right circumstances, he was the life of the party and funny. So why do we do it? Why do we buy into myths that we've created about our own nature, making us incapable of doing things we want to do?

It is important to get to your own truth and know that you have all the resources, skills and gifts to get to your dreams in life. Nothing has stopped me from reaching my goals. Even setbacks do not stop me. I look at every setback, analyze it and most importantly, I learn from it. Ask yourself after a setback:

• What was the lesson here?

• What will I do differently next time?

• How has this experience given me wisdom?

• How have I grown from this experience?

And when others see you after a setback and want to commiserate with you, immediately show them what a wonderful learning lesson it was.

Do not complain or whine.

Move forward, head up, chin high. And promise yourself not to define yourself by a setback. Remember, when something happens to you, the only thing that you have power over is how you choose to think about the situation. You can choose to find the value in it, or you can choose to incorporate it into your being and let it weigh you down. It's a simple choice. And the most beneficial approach is to see the value in it and throw away the rest of the baggage like clay around the sculpture. Keep the gift, toss out the garbage.

It is how we feel about things or events that can cause us pain. When we choose to see the value in every situation, we begin to move forward.

Powerful self-questioning will take you to action

When I ran for office at the age of 36, I went up against a former cabinet minister. I was relatively unknown, and yet I worked so tirelessly that the nomination race became very exciting and ignited people to get engaged in politics. The night the votes were counted and they announced the other woman as the victor, the strangest thing happened. I was washed over with the most wonderful feeling that here, the victory was not measured by votes, but there was something far bigger we had begun to embark upon for women. The events we hosted to advance women connected them with Lisa and with Nasima Nastoh whom you will read about in the chapter on **Justice**–these leaders who encouraged the many women in attendance make new connections to empower themselves–*was* the victory. Women left our events wanting to run for office, inspired to start their own companies and encouraged to trust that they are their children's first teachers. I knew that night the victory was not measured by the same rules others would apply. That is where we begin to find our own truths, to lead philosophically. And it was also a wonderful training ground to understand politics first hand.

I credit that experience in running for office for giving me the courage and insights to launch the first civic non-partisan society in the history of Nova Scotia. It was that experience and the research for this book, coupled with my experience in municipal government that empowered me to bring the idea of a civic society to like-minded Nova Scotians and to make it real. The Citizens for Halifax Society was launched on the 250th anniversary of democracy in Canada–in Nova Scotia where it all began. I could not have done this had I not ran for office. Looking back on this you can see that had I measured my run for office by the votes and not by the experience, I would never have been able to ignite Nova Scotians to build a healthy framework at the municipal level.

So the next time you take a risk and stretch, whether you run for office, start a company or reach out to your children and those around you, know that you may not meet the measure of success you were hoping for. But if you look deeper to see the true lesson or value, you may just find your success was higher than the measure of others. If you listen to that voice inside, that inner guide, you will see how that experience will lead you to the next step. And if you're not mindful of this, you may miss the true message or lesson altogether. Sometimes you really have to stretch yourself to begin to see the value when things don't go as you'd planned. But your own truth is there—you just have to look for it and you will find the lesson that will take you to the next level of your journey.

When Churchill was leading Britain and they were up against the brutal Nazis, there was a battle that cost the Allies a lot of men. His country came down hard on him, but Churchill refused to give up. He said, "We will fight and we will never surrender."

When the Allies finally won WWII, it was the strategy learned from the very battle they had lost, that helped them to win in the end. Can you imagine if Churchill had given up in the face of criticism? Can you imagine if he had not seen the true lesson in the tragedy?

Churchill did not give up; he did not surrender to scrutiny at home or the enemy abroad. That is a very, very important lesson for us to learn and live by.

Reflect on what the real lesson is in every one of your challenges in life and see the value in the learning so that you can move forward with your goals for right action.

No man is given more than he can bear.

– MARCUS AURELIUS

Our task is to summon the courage to be accountable as women and take responsibility for our own place in advancing the thinking of those around us. When we enlighten rather than condemn, we will advance ourselves in society. Ultimately, we will narrow the gap between rich and poor which is often the root of war and oppression.

Existentialism–choosing to interpret your circumstances

Man is Born Free

– JEAN-PAUL SARTRE

And the original line goes on to say, "...and everywhere he is in chains." Women are also born free. If you extend this idea to women, you will see that these self-imposed chains can be loosened and we can return to our birthright of freedom. For women and men living in a democratic society, this philosophy is an absolute truth.

Sartre showed us that we are certainly shaped by our experiences, whether we were raised poor, middle class or wealthy, whether we were born first or last or somewhere in the middle, and despite gender, culture, race, and religion, the kinds of mentors we had or didn't have, or the level of dysfunction in our families. Sartre acknowledged that these were our circumstances, and although these circumstances themselves cannot be changed or undone, we are all free to interpret them and give them meaning. This is my life's philosophy.

For me I believe the two greatest gifts I was given were being born poor and being born with a severe hearing impairment. My take on the condition of poverty, which I could not do a thing about until I could work at the age of 16, is that it taught me an incredible work ethic—a work ethic that I may not have been so quick to build upon if the "wolves weren't at the door." And the hearing impairment taught me to read people's body language. Body language makes up 70 per cent of what a person is really saying. So regardless of the words that I may or may not hear, I understand others very well through the way they communicate physically.

Now, I could have chosen to feel sorry for myself, as I couldn't change the fact that I was born poor and hearing impaired. However, as Sartre pointed out, I had the fullest freedom to interpret these experiences. Let me repeat this because it is so important. I had the fullest freedom to interpret the experiences of poverty and a severe hearing impairment. And I see them clearly as gifts that have contributed to my success and quality of life as an adult. We build ourselves out of our experiences and circumstances. We are free to give our past or current challenges new meaning—our own meaning. For example, if you became addicted to anything, whether it's smoking, alcohol, spending money or overeating, Sartre would argue that you live in a world that you, yourself, created through the meanings that you choose for events and circumstances. If you live with addictions, you have chosen this life, and you have the freedom to make the choice to live any other way you choose.

Sartre also said that you are not solely formed by your experiences—you are formed by the meaning you give those experiences. So if I had used poverty or my hearing impairment as an excuse for not excelling in life, it would have been my own choice to give those circumstances a negative meaning. I chose, however, and continue to choose, to see the value in both my childhood poverty and hearing impairment. I consider them both the greatest gifts I was given. I am not saying it was easy, but I am saying these gifts helped me to grow into the person I am.

As Sartre wrote in his play, *No Exit*, hell is other people—we mirror the people who surround us. I would like to add to Sartre's take on the power to give circumstances meaning, by discussing the importance of the people with whom you surround yourself. This impacts most things in your life.

When we were young, we chose our friends based on the schools we went to. Which school you attended depended on where you lived. As children, none of us had any control over where we lived; therefore, circumstances dictated both the school and the children who attended it. These schoolmates were not friends you would have selected necessarily—they were friends because of circumstance. However, once you moved away to work or went to university or college, your choice of friends did not depend on circumstances. You had full freedom to choose what kinds of people you wished to spend time with.

As an adult, you have the freedom to be with the people who support you. And now would be a good time to check in on the world you've created around yourself.

Ask yourself the following:

1. Are you surrounded by supportive people, including both mentors who teach you, and friends who believe in you?

2. Do you see the value in the circumstances that shaped you from childhood until now?

3. Do you see challenges as gifts?

4. Are you able to reach your goals?

If you're not able to reach your goals, it would be worth re-examining the way you interpret the circumstances of your past. Are you filled with negativity and fear? If so, you will want to find some new meaning from these experiences so that you can move forward. Another thing to check-in on is the kinds of people who you are attracting. If they are not supportive of your goals, you need to seriously reconsider the kinds of people you surround yourself with.

The evaluation we make about the people around us should not be based on status. This kind of evaluation cannot give a true picture of how they are a positive or negative in your life. A status-based evaluation would focus on a person's wealth, looks or popularity. A healthier check-in on the people you surround yourself with would be based on the following:

Do you surround yourself with people who:

• support you in your goals

• get excited about your accomplishments

• challenge you to be the greatest human you can be

• have high expectations of you and applaud you when you meet them

• make you laugh

• are there for you that one day out of 365 days of the year when you need them (otherwise, the other 364 days don't mean much if they can't come through on the one occasion that you call on them in need)

• back you up when in a challenging situation or unfair confrontation

• ensure you are not bullied or picked on

• listen to you

• find joy in your company

The meaning you give both your experiences and the people with whom you surround yourself will dramatically shape you and affect your outcomes.

I liken our journey to a flight path. If you go off just one degree for a long period of time, you can go way off course and into dangerous territory. If you control your flight path with clear goals and do the work to ensure you and your team are navigating with your co-pilot, your team will have a smooth, enjoyable journey with a good landing, regardless of the storms and turbulence that may come your way during the ride.

Existentialism

You have the power to live authentically

The philosopher, Jean-Paul Sartre, gave us existentialism. After WWII, it was all the rage to think like an existentialist because it symbolized personal liberation from the chains that bound people during wartime oppression.

Existentialism means having free will and being accountable for your choices, your interpretations and the meaning you choose to find in the world around you. What is so attractive about this aspect of the existentialist way of thinking, is that regardless of the point in time, post-war or not, humanity is always in a state of being bound by the chains of status. Existentialist philosophy works for us women today as much as it worked for the people of Paris in 1945 to rid themselves of the chains of oppression.

Sartre would challenge you to ensure you are not living in what he called "Bad Faith" that you are not living in the shadows, and lying to yourself about the world in which you live. Bad Faith, or "self-deception" is when we take no responsibility for who we are and the choices we make, when in fact, we are fully responsible for every one of our choices.

Bad Faith is when we pretend that we have no choices in life and we are forced to do things. Unless you are living under war-torn oppression like the women of Afghanistan, it is a farce to say that you are "forced" to behave in any manner which you know to be contrary to what you should be doing. This applies to your work and your personal life. When I hear someone say "My hands are tied," I just cringe. I can read it like a crystal ball: when someone says their hands are tied, I can pretty much predict they are spiralling downward and will experience very negative results from their actions—or lack of actions. When we live in Bad Faith, we take no responsibility for our actions and blame the circumstances with which we live for our outcomes. Remember, the last time you lived under circumstances beyond your control was when you lived with your parents and had to abide by their rules. Now that you are on your own, and presumably have been for quite some time, only you are responsible for the choices you make. *That is your truth.*

Sartre called our attempts to escape our own truths inauthenticity. So check-in and evaluate where in your life you may not feel that you are living authentically.

For me, my marriage broke down over eight years before I separated from my husband. We lived together, down the hall from each other, and yet I would take him out in public when I emceed an event and would force him to sit and chat with everyone and smile. We always argued before, after and during this charade, as it was really a big lie. We were living inauthentically. It was only when I checked in with myself and made the tough decision to leave, that I felt liberated and could see again. And so I packed my bags and he bought me out of our house that I had spent five years renovating. I took a loss financially, but I gained my freedom. All the chains that had bound me had been loosened, because I chose to finally break them. Only I had that power. This decision allowed me to go forward in other areas of my life. I began to evaluate my contracts and the next direction I would take. I realized that from all of my learning, I had a book to write. So I did it. And once I finished it, I began to explore the idea of a broadcast program and was asked to co-host on air and offers began to come in to host a show of my own.

Suddenly I was changing in so many ways. And I began to reflect: was I really changing, or was I just becoming honest with myself? I think you know the answer. So remember: when someone questions your changes, whether it be a job or divorce, or move, tell them you finally got honest with yourself.

Thanks to Sartre and existentialism!

When was the last time a woman friend said to you, "You are such an existentialist." When you were living honestly? Be that woman—that role model—the next time your friends do things that move them away from inauthenticity and towards living their own truth.

You know deep down what to do. When I was trying to leave my husband, I had a thousand excuses for why I could not leave. Were they true? Not at all. Did I think they were true? Absolutely. I was living the Bad Faith cycle that humans get caught up in because they don't want to disturb the status quo.

Remember, Marcus Aurelius, the greatest philosopher of all time, would remind you that you are dead in less than 100 years, so what is keeping you from living your own truth? No one is going to care that you left a bad marriage or a crummy job in 100 years, let alone next month. Trust me—I have done all of these things.

Walk with conviction, head high, chin up. People will only believe in your actions if you do.

Courage

All that is needed for evil to triumph is for good men to do nothing.

– EDMUND BURKE

Cowards and heroes are not born, they are defined in action.

– JEAN-PAUL SARTRE

S artre spent many years in companionship with the famous female philosopher, Simone de Beauvoir, who wrote *The Second Sex* and *Ethics of Ambiguity.*

One is not born, but rather becomes a woman.

– SIMONE DE BEAUVOIR

Essentially, Simone de Beauvoir brought to the forefront the realization that we must recognize our own freedom and define ourselves by our own terms rather than by the social expectations created by men.

If you had just one day left on this earth, you would bravely do anything you thought you needed to do with your time remaining. You would have the courage to fearlessly rectify the wrongs you see around you. Often we hear of stories where someone is diagnosed with a serious illness and, with no clear idea of how much time they have, they ensure they make good use of their time every single day while they can. Because there is a certain courage you summon from within when you know you have things you want to do on this earth and you have no idea how much longer you'll be around.

Story on life shifters

A 2003 issue of *BC Business Magazine* cover story will forever mark a significant turning point in my life. The story, "Life Shifters," covered six of us who had made drastic changes in order to live more authentic and fulfilling lives. The piece on my story told of how I had quit my job to start my company so that I would never have to compromise my ethics, and it also discussed my wish to spend more time with my children. My income more than tripled by making this life shift to being more authentic and being honest with myself about what it would take to lead the life that would give me the most meaning. The article moved many people, and I began to get calls from women and men seeking advice on how to make a similar shift in their own lives.

It was a request by David Jang that directed me into becoming a communicator on leadership. At that time, David was the organizer of a youth program called Student Street Squad, a program that empowers youth to be leaders in their communities. David asked if I would be a keynote speaker. I wrote back and said yes, as long as youth from all walks of life could attend. My concern was that I would only address the natural leaders who tend to follow the rules. I wanted to reach the students who didn't conform, for I felt they had some untapped magical and authentic leadership talent. David responded right away and was able to convince me that this was something I should do. It turns out he was right.

I prepared my presentation. I had never been a keynote speaker before and even more nerve-wracking was my secretive past that I was about to unleash. Of course, when I hit the part about how as children we had no socks in the winter and often went to school with no lunch that I began to choke back the tears and came close to crying. I regained my composure and provided context by adding that despite the hardship, I still went on to own my own company and live in beautiful British Columbia. It was this very true and honest talk that resonated with the youth. They related to the context of going from humble beginnings to achieving prosperity. I explained to them that nothing can keep you from living your dreams if you visualize it and work everyday on developing your character.

Your character is your destiny

I have done the presentation many times since then and I still come close to choking back tears each time. It's not easy to get up in front of 300 high school kids and tell them about visualization, using your own hard-knocks story as a real-life example. I can never shake the nerves before I get up for this presentation. And even though I speak at engagements frequently, the student presentation is always the toughest. It continues to be as challenging as it is rewarding, to deliver my ten-steps to visualization to youth. The thing that drives me forward is the notion that I might be speaking to a 15-year-old version of my younger self. This call to speak and the knowledge that I might reach one person who needs to hear a story they can relate to gets me past those insecurities. At every session, there has been at least one person who comes up to me at the end and says, "You were talking to me." And I say, "Yes, yes I was."

The youth understood clearly that nothing would stop me from my goals except for myself. They connected with this like it was news to them, and yet they readily received the information. In fact, incorporating the power of philosophy into the talk triggered the writing of this book. This was a very big and wonderful surprise to me—that this message would resonate so astoundingly with youth.

As I spoke of my studies in philosophy and credited the thinking of Plato, Sartre, and Marcus Aurelius in my life plan, the youth in the audience began to ask about studying the same great thought leaders.

It was one particular session that redirected and led me to the creation of *The 7 Virtues of a Philosopher Queen* workshop and book. One day, Nancy Campbell, a vice principal and wife of the Premier of British Columbia, Gordon Campbell, sat in the audience with her students. After the session, she approached me and asked if I would be a leader for a program called Minerva. I had never heard of Minerva and was most intrigued after researching it. I learned that it is a program geared towards getting women, aged 35–55, back in the work force after a hiatus. Whether they had taken time off to raise children or take care of parents, there were challenges in returning to the work force.

I was very honoured and was sharing this news with my good friend Rene, a self-described stay-at-home-mom. The conversation continued, and Rene shared with me how she frequently meets with other stay-at-home-moms (from now on we'll use the term work-at-home-moms since a mother's work is the most demanding job on earth). She told me how often these mothers would be reduced to tears trying to figure out how to get back on track in pursuing their lost dreams.

I realized then there were issues going on for women, regardless of whether they were in the work force or in the world of the work-at-home-moms, and that quick fix, band-aid solutions weren't working for us. I realized that we needed to connect with some of the powerful methodology that men have applied for centuries in work, business and government to give us more meaning and self direction. It was then that I began to piece together this program of philosophical empowerment for women.

I also realized how hungry working women were to connect with information that would help them with their family life—even when they were attending business seminars. I realized that we never turn off this desire to nurture our families, wherever we are. When I gave talks to women in business on economic development, I began to see that at the end of the sessions someone always asked me about my presentations to youth. Initially I wanted to avoid this subject and would immediately return to economic development. And then it dawned on me that the two are inseparable, that in order for women to advance their personal and professional lives, philosophical direction was something we all needed so we could ultimately integrate all aspects of our lives to lead *The good life.*

There are two chapters in the current story of women

I also came to the realization that you cannot separate women's work, whether it be at home or in the workplace, from our desire to lead our children and families. This was a eureka moment—for this is the core of how we can make the necessary changes in society. So here we have two chapters going on simultaneously in the building of our current *story of women*. On the one hand, we have the chapter of our professional lives, often trying to break through political, professional patriarchal barriers in order to advance the number of women in leadership roles. And on the other hand, the second chapter of our story occurs concurrently with the first: our sons and daughters are in dire need of our showing the way to a healthy, integrated society, workplace and political arena where men and women of philosophical direction are working towards the same shared goals.

And although we may not have the numbers to reflect this equality in our current work chapter, if we do not work towards ensuring our sons are provided with direction, the next generation of daughters will rule and there will be a backlash similar to that which the shift from a patriarchal society has triggered in Afghanistan. For the backlash in Afghanistan and in other countries is rooted in the empowerment of women. Women are connected to technology and learning and realize they deserve to study and become independent. This, in itself, is part of what's causing the shift from the patriarchal society and ultimately the backlash of oppression.

We must never stop educating ourselves as women and we must never be fearful of the backlash. However, we need to understand it and communicate effectively with each other and look out for our young sons.

We live in a society where it is not unheard of for a young, lost, male youth to ask himself whether he should become a rapper or join a terrorist group. This is serious indeed. As women, we are affected by this, and yet we have the power to shape and change this! This, again, is the *eureka* moment for us. We have the untapped power to ensure our young men are not lost or fall prey to organizations that would provide a false sense of direction and security. The philosophical mind cannot be manipulated by others.

If you do not know which direction you are going, someone else will direct you

We must realize that women are already leaders, but often we just need to reconnect with what we already know about ourselves, regardless of whether we are at home or at work. We need to reconnect with our former selves—who we were before husbands and children and daycare and soccer took precedence. I also recognize that there are many women in the work force who are not satisfied with their current work/life situation.

The dissatisfaction of women in the work force shows us that the fairy tale of what was expected of us socially still isn't coming together. And if indeed we get one go-a-round at this life, why would anyone not serve themselves and the people around them by working to their talents at all times for a meaningful life?

I also believe we must not lose our connection to our sons and daughters. Do not get lost in the obligations of work or the pressures of society. Stand by and for your children and let nothing keep you from showing them the way towards right action. Empowering your children to live the virtues comes first. After all, you are your child's first teacher.

Work to your talents

I am convinced that each of us already knows what we need to do to lead successful, meaningful lives. The answers are already within; we need not seek the answers from others. In fact, you could ask for advice from three close friends who know you really well and the odds are, each one of them will come up with a different solution for you. So why do we do it? Why do we continue to ask others what we should do, when we already have the answers? And would a man ask three friends what to do in a situation, whether professional or personal? More than likely, not.

Finding your answers starts with asking yourself questions.

- SOCRATES

The Socratic Method was named after the philosopher Socrates. When someone asked Socrates what they should do, he never gave them the answer; instead, he would ask a question back that would give the person the ability to ask themselves, in a reflective way, what to do.

It is a timeless, classic philosophy of the ancient philosophers—the belief that you already have the answers to your questions about life's meaning and purpose for you. To test its application, think back to when you were about eight years old. What was it that you so dearly wanted to become? Did you want to be the next Prime Minister? Perhaps you wanted to be a veterinarian, or a marine biologist or a business woman. Then what happened along the way that taught you that you could not live out the vision which seemed so clear to your eight-year-old self?

Why is it that at the age of eight, I knew what I wanted to be? Even though we didn't have socks in the winter, often went to school without lunch and many times weren't sure whose home we'd be going to for dinner after school, I knew what I wanted to be. And there was no part of my being that thought I would not achieve my goals. I saw myself as a business woman doing good things in the community. I could see a wooden door in the vision and I could feel the satisfaction of a life of great meaning. I felt **Courage**, **Wonder**, **Moderation**, **Truth**, **Justice**, **Wisdom**, and **Beauty** in my vision. I saw myself dressed professionally and working in the business world.

As I grew older, the vision got less clear. I could still see the wooden door and the power suit but the reasons for their part in the vision began to fog over. By the age of 18, I was convinced that it must have been the wooden door of my boss or my husband. The power suit could easily have been something an assistant to a leader would wear. And as the reason for the vision fogged over, so, too, did my ability to live out the vision until it was almost forgotten.

How then did I veer so far off track that I found myself university educated and pouring coffee to get my husband to his dream of becoming an engineer? I am convinced that at the isolated, naïve and innocent age of eight, I had the answers within and that somehow along the way, I became deployed by others and temporarily lost the ability to deploy myself. Now hold onto this thought as we work through the exercises later on in this book: to undo the negative deployment by others, we must be responsible and concurrently ensure we are conscious *not* to derail our children from their future quests.

Give yourself permission to speak up and take risks

When I was a young woman in my teens and early 20's I thought that men knew more than I did. I am not sure where I got this, but I grew fearful of speaking up for what I knew to be true. It was only as I began to observe men in positions of power making the wrong decisions and walking with conviction during those decisions that I began to realize I had an obligation to get over myself and speak up if I had important information to share with others.

I recall an interesting conversation I had with a male mayor I once worked for. He had lost his family fortune in a business deal that went bad. He never apologized, he did not wallow and he moved on to being elected mayor. After two terms he was voted out by the people and again he did not wallow, he did not apologize—he simply moved forward and rebuilt his company.

We talked about this experience. I observed that men like him do not apologize when disaster strikes. But they do learn from it. They learn not to repeat the same mistake, and they do not allow themselves to feel shame or guilt for having taken a risk. He agreed with my observation and added that this is how women deserve to live as well.

Because we were raised in a patriarchal society, it's as if we, as women, were not really given permission to make mistakes and simply learn from them. Or somehow we bought into the cultural teachings and told ourselves that we did not have permission to take risks. Either way, we must get over this and give ourselves permission to be courageous, take risks and take a stand for what we know to be true.

> *It is time to effect a revolution in female manners—*
> *Time to restore them to their lost dignity—*
> *and make them,*
> *As a part of the human species*
>
> – MARY WOLLSTONECRAFT

So stop and do the following check-in:

- Do you apologize when you make a mistake after having taken a risk?

- Or do you, instead, find the lesson in the experience and spring back and move on to the next decision to advance yourself with no apologies?

- Choose who you want to be. And then stand up for yourself and your children and be that brave voice.

This will be a challenging exercise as we have deep-seated judgments which we need to remove in order to extend a hand to our children. But it's doable. Recall the teenaged boy who dreamed of being a rapper who is now joining a terrorist group? Humans are not so different in the way we process information and this is where philosophical thinking will empower us with self-mastery for our own personal goals and those of the people we serve.

Reconnecting with the eight-year-old adult within

I learned from a Buddhist friend who believed that you become an adult at the age of eight. I immediately thought back to how clear my life's path had been at that age of eight and began to examine my life. I recall a certain feeling of courage and destiny that I possessed then, before it began to cloud over by others' influence as I grew older.

Remember, we are all capable of finding the leader within and leading a life of profound meaning and satisfaction.

Women, in particular, are born with the innate ability to use their intuition and multitask—skills necessary for leaders of businesses and organizations. In prehistoric times, women were the gatherers protecting their young while the males hunted. And while the males were away, women protected the young. We honed our instincts to sense anything that would hurt the ones we were in charge of.

Now in modern-day society, as the nurturers, we women often grapple with the social expectation of taking on a lesser role in the business and political world.

> *Justice itself is not the exclusive responsibility of any one class of citizens, but emerges from the harmonious interrelationship of each component of the society with every other.*
>
> – MARCUS AURELIUS

We learn in *The 7 Virtues of a Philosopher Queen* how the teachings in the humanities by the likes of Plato, Socrates, Marcus Aurelius, Mary Wollestonecraft, Simone de Beauvoir and Michaelangelo, can advance your life. You will begin to discover how to personally adopt their concept of the virtues so that you can make the connection between this ancient wisdom and its application to your own life.

Character is the benefit of building virtues within yourself. Your character will get you through any challenge, great or small.

If the virtues are the foundations of character, and your character is your destiny, then you can see the connection between building on the virtues and having a successful life—a life in which you define what it takes to live meaningfully while bringing happiness to those around you.

You don't have to tell any woman that if she gives, she'll get more in return. The question is how do we harness that sense of service with our other gifts of intuition and creativity to reap rewards beyond the satisfaction of being a caring mother, friend, boss, employee, entrepreneur or community member? How do we return to the dreams and vision we had before our current lives got in the way? Philosophy is the route to seeking justice for others and ultimate wisdom while personally benefiting from a successful life of meaning.

The need for more women to enter politics

One of the penalties of refusing to participate in politics is that you end up being governed by your inferiors

– PLATO

It takes Courage to enter Politics

I was told that politics can be referred to as a "blood sport." And yet for those who have a philosophical foundation in their lives, they walk through these distractions unscathed and untouched. Remember Churchill.

People enter politics for different reasons. Some, like Churchill, enter to serve. Others enter for power and to understand more on this model, Machiavelli's book, *The Prince,* shows how some leaders believe it is all about power.

For those who go into politics to serve—this is the highest level of service. Recognizing that you have a skill at communicating the rights of others and entering government with that goal, is a noble and courageous thing to do.

And when you enter politics to serve, you must understand that you will come up against those who are in it for power. And this is where you must muster up all the courage you can imagine to stay the course and remain true to yourself and let nothing stand in your way of serving the greater good.

Women in politics

Until philosophers rule as kings or those who are now called kings and leading men genuinely and adequately philosophise, that is, until political power and philosophy entirely coincide, while the many natures who at present pursue either one exclusively are forcibly prevented from doing so, cities will have no rest from evils,... nor, I think, will the human race.

- PLATO, *The Republic*

It is a strange reality for us, as women, when we examine where we are in politics. We have had the right to vote for less than 100 years. And today 52 per cent of the voting power in Canada is held in the hands of women. That means we, as women, have the power to collectively vote in a direction that could support the leadership of our government at every level. Governments can rise and fall completely at the hands of the collective vote of women—that is a lot of voting power. And yet, we have only 20 per cent representation. This means only one out of every five politicians is a woman. This means we are not represented equally.

Where have we given up our power?

In Plato's *Republic,* he showed us that if we are to truly get a clear picture of the right way to live for the individual, we must look at the state. Plato gave us the following questions which are important for any woman considering a life in politics:

What is the good society?

What is power and control and whose hands should they rest in?

What is our relationship as individuals to government?

Plato examined the justice of the soul. He showed us the soul has its three parts living in harmony. He likened the city to the individual and showed us that cities are as healthy as the people who run them. So those individuals who lead a life of philosophical direction have an obligation to enter the polis (politics) to ensure the health of the city or government is maintained. Once we shift the culture to one that encourages women to pursue the call to serve in politics, then our individual thinking will shift and more women will get into office so that we can foster networks connecting all levels of our society. You will see more on this in the chapter on Justice and the model of economic development that shifts away from the competitive nature of the patriarchal society to a more consensus-building model that holds the interests of women and men in a state of equal representation.

Plato showed us that when human appetites take over the elements of the intellect and reason, evil can prevail. Therefore, it is vital that women who can make the connection among service, reason and the rights of all classes of people enter politics in order to create a more balanced, realistic representation for everyone.

I believe the thing preventing women from going into politics most is fear. Fear is the biggest deterrent for many women when entering politics. One way to overcome this fear is to recognize that if you do feel the call to serve in government, you have an obligation to forget yourself and your ego and focus upon the people that are counting on your wisdom to do the right thing. You also have an obligation to yourself to live according to your true nature and if the call to serve in government continues to come up for you, then you must explore how best to answer this call.

A study was done on the barriers for women entering municipal government—the level of government that applies to cities, towns and regions. The paper, entitled "Untapped Resources; Women and Municipal Government in Nova Scotia," can be applied to any city in Canada as our numbers of women representatives are very similar. I will reference this study throughout this section on politics, for the findings were enlightening and some of the answers to their posed issues will be found in the following pages.

You will also get first-hand insights from several women who entered politics from interviews throughout this chapter. These women are from different political parties of which I will not mention and I will keep this non-partisan so that we may focus upon their wise words and lessons and use them as a learning guide for all women interested in learning more about politics.

At the United Nations Beijing Conference on Women and Decision Making, findings were established that female representation must hit at least 30 per cent to ensure the concerns of women are addressed in government. This will be our "tipping point," just hitting 30 per cent. We are currently at 20 per cent representation—that means this next ten per cent is crucial in making the big change we need to see in North American society. This is a very important benchmark that we can get to, and you can have a role in accelerating us to this number. Read on and learn how.

Remember what Plato said: "One of the penalties of refusing to participate in politics is that you end up being governed by your inferiors." Being governed by your inferiors is far more frightening than stepping up and entering the political arena.

I have had the pleasure of meeting many great women in politics at the municipal, provincial and federal levels of government. Each one of them has a certain strength, a conviction that they can make a difference. They are often able to speak the language of politics and business, which is crucial in this world.

So where do you begin?

Demystifying government

In Canada we have three levels of government: municipal, provincial/ territorial and federal. Whether you are thinking of entering politics, or working in the worlds of business or non-profit, or simply want to understand the value of your vote, it is crucial that you understand the very basics of government.

When we were in school and they explained the three levels of government, I somehow missed the context or meaning of it, for it was not explained in a way that was real or connected to my reality of the world.

Over time, as I began to meet my Mayor, my Premier, my MP, did I make the real connection between what these people do to serve us and how best to understand where they fit into our lives. This first-hand experience with political officials is the best way to understand government and to get excited about it because you are immersed in the energy and possibility of it all.

There are many ways to explain Canada's three levels of government. I am best able to do this based upon my own experience. A complete description of Canadian government would be a book in itself, so what follows are just a few key things you should know.

> **Municipal:** Served by a Mayor, and Councillors, and School Board members (in rural areas the Mayor is sometimes called the Warden or the Reeve).

> **Provincial or Territorial:** Served by a Premier, Cabinet Ministers and MLAs (Members of the Legislative Assembly).

> **Federal:** Served by the Prime Minister, Cabinet Ministers, MPs (Members of Parliament) and Senators.

With the exception of Senators (who are appointed), these representatives are all elected by us at three different elections. Municipal Elections take place every two to four years, depending on where you live. Provincial and Federal elections usually take place every four to five years, however they can happen more frequently in the case of minority governments.

You have a variety of these elected officials in your community. In order to understand who to deal with on which issues, their key roles are as follows.

Municipal Government governs a City, Town or Region. It is the most grass-roots level of government. Personally I believe this is a very accessible level of government, for it's so easy to connect with and get action for the people. The City state is the area that Plato looked at in *The Republic*. The City government of today deals with issues of zoning, by-laws, local police and planning. The City is responsible for your civic buildings, from city hall to your recreation facilities, most parks, to your library and some social services.

The biggest challenge facing the modern-day city is urban decay, as the rural areas are depleting and people are moving into urban centres. Eighty per cent of the population in North America dwells in urban centres. The need for keeping up with this growth and ensuring that we are providing opportunities for the less fortunate in healthy and responsible ways, can be seen in the streets.

Panhandling, graffiti, crime, poverty and homelessness are a measure of the city's health. The healthier the city, the lower the level of urban decay you will find.

Provincial or Territorial Government governs a province or a Territory. The concerns of the Premier and the MLAs are provincial. They deal with issues around transportation, education, health care and most social services. Provincial responsibilities include highways, schools and hospitals. They are often responsible for some major parks as well.

Federal Government governs the country. The concerns of the Prime Minister, Cabinet Ministers, MPs and Senators centre around things like criminal law, taxation, monetary policy, banking, broadcasting, defense, immigration and social programs like employment insurance and the Canada Pension Plan. The Federal Government is also involved with major infrastructure projects, ports, airports, national and historic parks and other countrywide concerns.

All three levels of government are concerned with economic development and the overall health and welfare of its citizens. It is important that your representatives are all working together with a shared goal.

Remember, you get to vote for all three levels of government. You have the power to tell your elected officials whether you like what they are doing or not with the simple stroke of a pencil on your ballot.

You have even more power in telling them whether you like what you see by supporting someone you believe in who is running for office, or even by running yourself.

The American system

In the United States there are also three levels of government: local, state and federal. The local governments have a similar role to Canadian municipal governments.

State governments are different from Canadian provincial/territorial governments in several ways. A state has a governor (like a premier) but its cabinet members are not elected legislators as is the case in Canada. A state legislature usually has two houses, compared to a single house in Canadian provinces. The role of a state includes responsibility for criminal law and banking, which are federal roles in Canada.

The American federal Congress looks similar to Canada's parliament in that it has two houses. However, American congresswomen and congressmen are elected every two years. In Canada Senators are appointed and hold office until they turn 75, but in the U.S. they are elected for six-year terms.

This barely scratches the surface of the American system.

Training for running for office

Plato built the academy to train leaders with a foundation in philosophical thinking. Plato created an intellectual and spiritual environment where the prime goal was to train humans with primarily ethical aims. He taught people to live with philosophical direction so that they could lead fairly. The students worked on transformation of the self and transformation of the city.

Women in Canada first got the right to vote in provincial elections in 1916, in Manitoba, Alberta and Saskatchewan. Women were not able to vote Federally until 1918. It was not until 1929 that women were legally declared "persons" and were allowed to become members of the Senate. And it was not until 1940 that women in Quebec were given the vote. Hundreds of women have since gone into government in Canada.

Although women have made great strides since getting the vote Federally in 1918, we still only have 20 per cent representation in Federal politics in Canada. Wales became the first jurisdiction to elect 50 per cent women, ahead of Sweden at 45 per cent women representation. These progressive countries have been accredited for having financing and electoral reform to support women entering politics. Democracies with proportional representation have on average twice as many women in office.

Remember, the United Nations Beijing Conference on Women and Decision Making established that it would take a 30 per cent bare minimum for governments to be responsive to the needs of women. Quebec is the only province that is meeting this minimum requirement in provincial government. On average political representation is still at 20 per cent women for the rest of Canada.

How do we get into office?

This is a very good question that has a process. First of all, it helps to learn the language of those in government. Once you have begun to lead philosophically and have the concern of the greater good, you must get involved in supporting other great leaders.

Let's start at the very beginning–Municipal Level

An interview with Diane Thorne, who was a Municipal Councillor and who went on to become a Provincial MLA in British Columbia, shared some insights on where to begin.

Diane's Story

In an interview, Diane shared her view that women interested in a life of service in politics should begin at the Municipal level for "thousands of good reasons," as she put it.

"I think women should go for the Municipal level first. There's no end to the reasons for this. It is close to home for your first foray into politics. The comfort is there. And remember, when you enter politics, you don't have to win to enter. Whether you win or lose, your life will never be the same. You will be treated differently; people will know who you are and what you stand for.

"Secondly, it's grass-roots politics. You get to know the community which is important when you go further up to other levels of government.

"And thirdly, because you are local, you get a lot more publicity. You achieve phenomenal name recognition at the Municipal level. This is essential to move up to the senior level. That's why I unseated the MLA in my riding.

"You're safe and comfortable and you're learning and you're achieving anything you set out to do if you begin with running for City Council."

Even though Diane Thorne and I belong to different political parties—which means some of our values and what we stand for are not the same, we got to know each other and could call upon each other for things we needed in order to serve our community. I have seen first hand that women have a real gift for getting beyond partisan politics and I think this gift can serve us in advancing and getting more women into government. If we can get beyond our differences and see where the lessons and learning are, we will hit that benchmark of 30 per cent representation.

Diane's Perspective

Diane Thorne answered some questions during our interview that address some of these burning questions.

We own 52 per cent of the vote and yet, only 20 per cent of the seats in office in Canada are female. The Beijing United Nations report said we need at least 30 per cent representation to ensure the issues that are relevant to women get appropriate attention. Are we moving forward on this?

"The numbers of women in office are going down," says Diane Thorne. "It is going to take a concerted effort by everyone to get more women into politics. It is going to take men and women. Men are going to have to recognize that they have to step back in order to get the numbers up for women. Men have paid lip service to this, and now the time has come for action, to put women in seats that are winnable. I also think there may be men who are saying 'women do not like the *rough and tumble* of politics.' Women don't say those things—men say them. I think women have bought into this and have come to see this as their reality and it's *not*. It's insidious because it seems to be so caring.

"Not liking the *rough and tumble* is not the reason women do not get elected. Women cannot get nominated in a winnable riding. Men simply woo and recruit men who are winnable and put them in a winnable riding. Then these men can say they did their best to get women into office but they really have not. Every party has that trait. To excuse the lack of action shows that we, as women, have bought into this myth."

What soft and loving woman would want to come into this brutal world of politics?

"When you talk about politics, from the school board up to Ottawa, there is nothing to stop a person from running—it seems very simple. The solution is easy—yet men won't give up some of the power. It is a yin and yang situation. Men have to begin to give that up willingly in order to make room for women in politics. And yet I don't see them lining up to say, *you can have my seat.*"

What did you see happening or not happening that ignited your interest in politics?

"Originally in the 90's, when I was 53, I got elected to City Council. I ran because I thought it was time for council to have women. At the time there was only one woman on our City Council and I felt there needed to be a voice for our interests. We desperately needed the female perspective, but also were in need of a progressive way to make decisions which would move the community forward. I saw things that were *not* happening but needed to happen.

"They needed a progressive woman's perspective."

You had a municipal seat and then went provincial—what is the biggest difference going from municipal to partisan politics for you?

"Just being a partisan politician was huge. The biggest difference is that in municipal government, you are a non-partisan politician. You can express your beliefs, your values, your issues, you never have to worry about stepping over any lines. You never have to clear it with anybody because you do not belong to a party.

"When you step up to the senior levels, you can never make it as an independent politician. You have to belong to a political party because you need the backing. You need the help and you need the support from your chosen party. Hopefully you are able to be a member of a party you believe in that aligns with your values.

"I feel that I am connected to my party and I want other women to think about that. It is important when you do run at a senior level of government and you are a member of a party, that at least your values match the majority of the values of the party you are with.

"And there are two key reasons for this.

"The first is personal and it's very important for my peace of mind that I do believe in the majority of the things that my party believes in. And I think that makes me a better politician, because I can tell the truth and that's what people want.

"Second is for the political process for the party, because you can have a candidate who will run for a party because it's opportune, not because they've examined the values of the party. Then you have a possible winner who is not authentic and may not know the values later and then you have people leaving their parties.

"It is important that you feel at home. I would never cross the floor. I know what I stand for. So the difficult part is when I don't agree with the party."

What do you believe we can do to get closer to equal representation, by that I mean that many women find politics to be intimidating, yet you get right in there. So what things have you done to look at politics from a different perspective, a less intimidating place?

"The key thing that allowed me to run for politics was to learn how to do public speaking. I was terrified of it. I went through my twenties and did tons of modeling. The public eye never bothered me. I always loved being the centre of attention, but I never opened my mouth. I was afraid of ridicule. So I went into my thirties and realized this was the only thing I needed to get over and it was my Achilles heel. I believe everyone has one but they never deal with it. And I have never been a person to deal with denial.

"In 1968 when I was 25 years old, I discovered politics. Pierre Elliott Trudeau had entered the scene and I became a Trudeau groupie. He ignited that interest for me and when I started to mature, in my thirties, I did two things; I took on public speaking because I knew it was my Achilles heel and I finally had children. I think you can't be truly successful and have peace of mind if you don't face your Achilles heel and deal with it, climb over it, learn how to break it into pieces, just get over it. I stood in front of crowds and sobbed. This was through the group Toastmasters. I was honest with myself. I now listen to my inner voice in the end. I don't listen to anybody else's voice. But I do like to learn from others."

And that is why Diane is a success.

A new kind of community involvement for women
In the executive association of your riding

My Rotary Club mentor was Irene Barr. She has inspired so many women to get engaged in government at various levels, and has shared some insights on what to do to get elected. Irene was the president of the Women's Commission for her provincial party. She said one of the first things to do with provincial and federal office is to get involved in the executive of your riding association.

This means you have chosen the party you believe in, the one which has demonstrated leadership and is a group of people who share your philosophical convictions. Once you have done so, you join that party. So you get a membership form and you become a member of the party. Then you begin to volunteer for the party and share your interest in running for the party executive and ask the good questions, make observations and ensure you are supported by good people within the party.

Some women are very good at supporting each other in running for office. There are groups of women who will host potluck dinners and take care of each other's children while other women are out door-knocking. I believe this is one of the most important things you can do to support a woman—and we do not see enough of this. Running for office means sitting at people's kitchen tables often late at night, learning more about their issues and what they need to see happen in government. If you have young children, having the supports in place so you can freely campaign, is one of the most important things you can do. If you know of a woman whom you would like to see run, the finest thing you can do for this woman is to organize supports for her family so that she can go out and run the best campaign possible. There is no lack of desire for women to run for office—there just needs to be support from the team surrounding her that will ensure she can campaign well.

There are many other important aspects to running a solid campaign: buttons, t-shirts, stickers, signage, Web site, PR, Campaign Manager, fundraising and the list goes on. But none of these is as important as having the family supports in place from the start.

Insights on where to begin—Untapped Resources—a report

The philosophers believe you have all the resources you need to lead the good life. Often it is a matter of identifying where those resources are and how to access them. It is important to note that nothing can keep you from making *your* dreams a reality—only you. Having said that, it is important to see what the true obstacles are so that we can drive around them, go under them, and ultimately, *get over them*. And most importantly, when you see a "hurdle," you do not see it as something that can stop you, instead you examine it and figure out which way to go past it.

I was very fascinated when I read *Untapped Resources: Women and Municipal Government in Nova Scotia*. My cousin, Andrea Doncaster, was the Chair of the YWCA board when this study was commissioned and kindly forwarded a copy when she learned about my book. The information contained in the study is important for it truly does represent most of Canada and much of North America in terms of the obstacles out there and the self-imposed cultural learning which allows us to keep ourselves out of politics. The study used information from initiatives from across Canada and around the world to draw its conclusions.

The study revealed that women are lacking appropriate representation, although women make up more than 50 per cent of the population; under 22 per cent of municipal councillors, 7 per cent of wardens and mayors, and only 14.5 per cent chief administrators (the lowest in Canada).

Why is it important for women to participate in Municipal Government?

As you read Diane Thorne's story, she felt her city was not being progressive enough and it was not moving forward with the times. She knew that at the Municipal level, she could effect change if she had a seat at the table. And so she ran for Council and won.

The philosopher Plato, would argue that service in the City is the obligation of the Philosopher Queens and Kings.

So if you have issues in your city, whether you feel you are losing talented young people to urban centres or there are not enough jobs or opportunities, then you need to talk to your Municipal leadership, at the political and staff level. At the opposite end of the spectrum, if you feel your city is growing at a pace where the city is not managing its growth and crime is on the rise, you must again speak up and get involved and be a part of the solution. If you have insights on how to make these improvements, then you must get involved. It's as simple as picking up the phone and calling City Hall to learn more about the ways to get involved. And just, maybe, after you have learned more about the mechanics of it, you will go further and run for office, or at least ignite other women with the desire to run.

When women are not consulted, they are not at the table. Then the decisions affecting us get made without us. We can collectively reverse this situation, as it is our responsibility to seek out the answers to engage in the health of the City.

The "Untapped Resources" study revealed that women tended to be clustered in clerical positions where they "wield little influence," as opposed to management, in which only 29 per cent were women and only 14.5 per cent were the City Managers or Administrators.

We also learned that women made up less than one-third of the members of boards and commissions. And when women did sit on boards, they were clustered on recreation and heritage boards and not on the boards which make decisions about finance, land use, planning and public safety. So I put it to you, *How can a single mom buy milk at night and feel safe in an urban setting if all decisions surrounding the issues that underlie urban decay, have few, if any, women at the table?* Economic development committees which deal in finance, land use and planning and public safety, need more women.

When I go to an Economic Development Conference, I see approximately 75 per cent Caucasian males, and have seen few, if any representatives from the multicultural dynamics of our communities. This is why we continue to have children living in poverty. Unless the people who understand the issues of immigration and women's issues have a seat at the table where economic development decisions are made, we will continue to have an unacceptable level of people living below the poverty line.

I sat on the Economic Development Committee for my city in British Columbia and worked on building the model of economic development and found it so exciting. I made it exciting because I saw that single mom as clear as day. I never lost sight of her counting on me to be there–to represent her. It is the idea of the single mom or recently landed immigrant that drove me to ensure I spoke on their behalf.

When I first attended an Economic Development Committee meeting I must admit, I was nearly bored to tears and no one liked my new ideas. But I remained. I saw that single mom in my mind, and she was counting on me. After four years, I was able to bring about change and the Committee had become re-energized with a healthier perspective and everyone enjoyed what we'd accomplished in reversing the ills of urban decay. And after bringing home five national marketing awards from the Economic Developers Association of Canada for the implementation of ideas that represented people who had previously not been represented, we were able to change the course of the Economic Development Committee to include the socio-economic development that concerned women, youth, and our immigrants.

Imagine if I had let the boredom of people who were involved for the wrong reasons deter me from staying the course. Many people have come and gone and I was still standing after years of re-energizing the Committee with new perspective, suggested solutions and having the will to say we can do better.

And there is no compromising. The developers and the seniors can agree. There does not need to be conflicting interests as I have learned first hand on our revitalization project.

So if it's that easy, why aren't more women involved?

The "Untapped Resources" study revealed the following main reasons why women don't fully participate in municipal decision making. Remember, this is the place recommended as the starting point in politics for women, so if we can't get excited about this, it's just never going to happen for us. So I want you to really look at the following revelations from the study.

1. **Awareness of Municipal Government:** Most women and men don't recognize the importance of municipal government in our day-to-day lives.

2. **Appreciation of the importance of having different perspectives** in decision making. The more like-minded a group is, the less likely they are to make decisions that consider the needs of people unlike them. Women's experiences and socialization are different from those of men, just as the experiences of African Nova Scotian women differ from those of Mi'kmaq or Caucasion women and wealthy women's experiences differ from those of low income women. We need to see ourselves reflected in an institution before we can believe that it is relevant to us. For these reasons, women—in all their diversity—must have input.

3. **Women need to earn an income** to support themselves and their families. Those with paid employment find that hours of work or workload can conflict with Council work. Councillors who attended the focus groups had retired before running for office were self-employed or had other sources of income. This appeared to be less of a problem in the largest municipality where they are paid for full-time work.

4. **Women are busy.** Focus group participants echoed research from Statistics Canada showing that women still

perform most of the caring and household management
in addition to paid employment and voluntary work.

**5. Women often don't have equal access to
household assets** such as vehicles and the Internet, and
they are more likely than men to be poor.

The study went on to show that although women are busy and may
lack resources, they do get involved in community, church and other
volunteer organizations. So why aren't women involved as much in
municipal government? Below are some of the reasons cited from
the study in bold type. You will find some observations drawn from
the philosophers and the interviews I held that may shed some light
on the potential solutions to these cited challenges. And that is what
we hope to achieve here, to establish potential solutions to these findings.

The philosophers would remind us that we have *all* the resources we
need available to us. We just need to look at them in more creative
ways in order to identify them. We need to use the virtue of wonder
rather than doubt in coming up with the resources and solutions to
the challenge of getting more women into office. Remember, many
hands make light work, and you do not have to take this on alone. For
this reason men have formed solid networks and it's time for women
to learn from men what is good about their leadership style.

Untapped Resources Report

• **Many women have given up on Municipal Government as
a way of making change. The United Nations Beijing Conference on Women and Decision Making determined that a
critical mass of about 30 per cent is needed before governments are responsive to women. This is a wake-up call to
governments not only to include women, but to diligently
seek out their input and listen to them.**

This was a very important piece of information for me. Up until now
I had tried to see how we could get equal representation. I and many
of my peers were working toward 50 per cent representation. Knowing that the "tipping point" is just 30 per cent representation, I feel
the first wave of change is merely ten per cent more representation

of women in government and I know we can obtain this—and then keep going for 50 per cent. I also feel this is a wake-up call to women, not just government. For we need to see our own opportunities differently—we have all the resources we need to enter office, we just need to identify them. Waiting for government to do this is not acceptable. In the end, it is entirely up to women to be heard.

- **Elected women commented that personal, institutional and public expectations regarding their responsibilities as elected officials sometimes conflicted and competed with personal, spousal and societal expectations of their care giving and household management responsibilities. Institutional constraints often made this even more difficult, for example, when meetings were scheduled at times when women were busy making dinner and supervising their children's homework.**

While earning my second university degree, I took night courses and did not have a partner, as my son's dad was living and working in Alberta. I hired babysitters, even though I was making below poverty-level wages, and managed to attend my classes. Now that I am better off financially, I attend many evening meetings at City Hall as well as networking events, and I still hire a sitter or have their step-dad care for them.

Who said that a mother had to be home at 7:00 p.m. every single night? Where in this mythical "rule book of life for mothers" does it state this?

Where did we ever get the idea that we had to do everything for our children every single night? Let go of any preconceived notions of who has to be home and when. Whether you are studying in university, working or sitting on a committee or City Council, you must give yourself, as a mother, permission to be outside the home at hours that are sometimes in the evening. It's more than OK. Why would being on City Council be any different? Many things take us outside the home after 7:00 p.m. at night. We have no problem organizing a baby shower or an engagement shower or a church fundraiser at 7:00 p.m. on a week night.

Everyone will get used to it. It's change, but once you begin, you will see that it's no different than your child's right to go to school at 9:00 a.m. We have to shift the culture and our way of seeing things and it begins with allowing yourself to go out and do the things you need to do when you feel the call to do them. Slow cookers are great—throw everything in at 7:00 a.m. and put it on low and when everyone comes home—voila—dinner is ready. Is anyone going to get broken up if it's not you ladling the stew out of the slow cooker for them? Everyone will adapt.

There are ways to get around the issues cited above. Homework can be done by the sitter or father, or children can assist each other. Or you can do it at 3:00 p.m. Often we do our homework at 5:30 p.m. before my meetings. Remember, these meetings are *not* every night. This is once a week or twice a week maximum. Your family can do without you for an evening or two a week. We also do not overwhelm ourselves on the weekend. We are not running from lessons to sports to more functions. We sleep in on Saturdays and watch cartoons together.

We also have to recognize that our children live by our example. When we live authentically and independently, they witness this and it shapes them in positive ways that can compliment the academic studies they pursue in school. We have to see our children's learning as extending beyond traditional school and it encompasses us demonstrating to them that you can make a difference and that parents can realize their dreams and our children will learn this by osmosis when we demonstrate this in our daily lives.

Giving birth to our "ideas" is as important as giving birth to our children. Socrates pointed this out as well. The philosophers would have you ensure you live creatively and implement ideas that can better the lives of the citizens around you. We must begin to give our ideas a new and higher level of value.

- **Campaign financing was also reported as a factor in the "Untapped Resources Report" affecting women's ability to compete for elected office. Many of the elected women noted that with no ceiling on campaign spending, those with sources of financing had the advantage.**

Women are excellent at fundraising. There is no end to the amount of fundraising we do for our schools and non-profits. Pull that talent and expertise over to a campaign with the same passion for a cause and you will meet success. Raising money for your own political campaign is a snap. Just rent the town hall, put on a dinner, get some silent auction items from your friends and you've got $5,000 to start your campaign. Enlist all your friends who are in sales to assist you on your fundraising team. I know because I have done this—it is not difficult and lack of funding or financing is by no means a good enough excuse not to run for office.

- **In the focus groups for the report, women noted that female candidates with prior political experience and connections to political parties appeared to have an advantage over those without the contacts and experience running in a campaign.**

And they were correct. You absolutely have to have some level of political experience. This also extends to men. There is no getting around this, regardless of gender or socio-economic status. You cannot expect to go into any arena, particularly the political arena without some experience. And it costs nothing. Anyone can do it. Volunteering is the best way to start. Find someone you admire in politics and get out and support him or her. This is how you form the all-important network. I promise you, when you call the office of your favourite politician, the staff will find you some exciting volunteer work and you will be enjoying a BBQ in their backyard in short order.

- **Social expectations regarding "appropriate" behaviour for women appears to be a catch-22 in the political arena. Many women Councillors said it can take years for them to have credibility and be accepted by their male counterparts. Several described not being accepted until they became "one of the old boys," suggesting that they had to conform to the behaviour and culture of the male-dominated Council. At the same time, women often get criticized for doing this. Many women who attended the Women in Local Government focus groups sessions, including municipal politicians, expressed a dislike for aggressive behaviour and disrespectful language which sometimes occurs in Council meetings.**

This is an important piece of information. For the philosophers would have you cast off any concern of what others think of you. Men have done this for centuries. Men do not care what people say about them. Women pay too much attention to what others say. As for becoming one of the "old boys," that is the last thing we should do. Having said that, you must learn the language so that you can effectively communicate with them. There is a big difference between becoming an "old boy" and being able to communicate effectively with one. Once women understand this, they will be able to navigate the waters of political office much better. As for aggressive behaviour and disrespectful language, none of it can affect you if you choose to let it wash off your back. Remember, why would you care about the opinion of someone who knows not where they are going? You need only be concerned with the direction *you* are going in and the people you serve. Stay the course and stay true to your work and remove yourself of your ego. Take *nothing* personally and continue to serve the people who are counting on you to be strong for them.

- **There was also discussion around the adversarial nature of politics, with its winner-take all, "majority rules" approach to decision-making. Women may prefer to work towards consensus.**

As we shift out of the patriarchal society, take solace in knowing that with more women, certainly when we hit the "tipping point" of 30 per cent and we are only ten per cent away from that, there will be more collaborative methods of reaching consensus. We are very close to obtaining this kind of consensus-building style of leadership we just need to reach the "tipping point" of 30 per cent representation. So if for the short term we could attract women with the promise that it's on the horizon, then those women of philosophical direction will enter and pave the path for other women, and we will enjoy a new kind of leadership which is more attractive to women. But we will never get there if we don't hit that "tipping point." So waiting for it to happen is not an option.

The nomination race–Provincial and Federal candidate hopefuls

When you do decide to run at the Provincial or Federal level of office, hopefully you have already enjoyed some time as an elected official at the Municipal level of government as advised by Diane Thorne. The Nomination race is an internal race at both the Provincial and Federal levels of government. This is where a party holds an internal race, with all the people running who want to be the candidate for their party; so they are all running against people who belong to the same political party. The person who wins goes forward and runs against candidates from the other parties to obtain a seat.

I have had the great honour of being mentored by incredible human beings including Irene Barr from my Rotary Club in British Columbia. Irene Barr was the president of the Women's Commission in BC for her party. She shared some profound first-hand experiences which provide some perspective on how similar the situation is for women across North America. No matter where we live, the issues are the same and therefore the solutions are the same.

Irene pointed out that in her run for office at the Provincial level of government it was difficult to get the riding association's support and that hurt her run for office. She advised women to get engaged in the riding association, whether Provincial or Federal, before they run for office. This support is very important in the race for office. Here is what Irene had to say on the subject.

"My advice for women is that they see their nomination race as needing the support of both men and women. You will be looked at for your skill set and you should not feel you have a special place because you are a woman. Women are falling behind because women do not take the time to get into the riding where they are running at least two years before the nomination race. Build a relationship with the riding and the party so that you are known and you can be supported for your position and the work you have performed. You should bring your own team into the riding association so they see the support you have behind you before you announce your interest in running, and lastly, you need to have an excellent campaign manager and fund-raiser."

I would like to add to Irene's comments that men do these things as well as women who are connected, and the odds of meeting success are far higher when you follow this strategy.

Irene went on to discuss the nomination race:

"I think that women need to get used to the 'race.' The nomination race is one of the most difficult and often brutal experiences you could find. Women have to realize that they must sign up genuine support, and the number of people you sign up is the only thing that matters at this level of running for office. Women often do a soft-sell approach, and that just does not work. Signing up members to any party is a difficult task, and men can often tap into networks of "old boys" who blindly sign up for their buddies. Women are more thoughtful when they support someone and, therefore, are more reluctant to jump in. Most of the women who succeed have a strong group of male support as well as female support."

This is the most crucial bit of information. Remember, the philosopher Jean-Jacques Rousseau, wrote *The Social Contract* in the 1700s, and he revealed that in the natural state men are of a competitive nature and have to form networks to ensure they don't go into the natural state of war with each other. As a result, for centuries men have forged solid networks with each other in order to advance in business and government. I surmise that women, who are naturally collaborative, have not felt this need to form a network. In order to enter politics you must recognize the importance of the network and get networked with smart men and women so that you can meet success in running for office.

When asked if she felt that we are making strides forward, Irene responded:

"No, I think we are going backwards. We need more women who have been successful in being elected to office, to reach out and mentor other promising women candidates. We need to ensure that we put forward the best candidate by preparing women for the race.

"The undercurrent of each nomination can be a difficult battle. Sometimes the most influential members of a riding association have selected someone they wish to see have the nomination even though there are a number of good candidates both men and women seeking a nomination. This preference can influence the vote. It is important that women considering running for a nomination are aware that sometimes background activities are taking place. Women can succeed by demonstrating their open and honest efforts and by following the tried and true method of gaining a nomination and that is to sign up qualified members."

On learning the language of competition

The delicate dance will be to understand the language of competition and sport and yet at the same time, play the game on fair terms. I am convinced this will happen when we hit the 30 per cent "tipping point." In the meantime, it is crucial to understand that until we have hit that tipping point, we will continue to walk in a world of business and government shaped by patriarchal networks of a competitive nature. And consensus-building in government and politics will happen once we increase our numbers. So the challenge to you, the Philosopher Queen, is to strip yourself of your ego, get networked, learn the language, and stand firm on your mission. With that, you will meet success and ultimately pave the way for more women to enter government. Once you are inside, make it your work to ignite the enthusiasm and interest of others and work to support them to make positive change.

The great philosopher, Plato, would go so far as to say that one cannot become a leader, certainly not in a political arena, until one has truly understood and begun to live the virtues.

> *Philosophy enables us to discern what is just for a City or an individual in every case and the human race will have no respite from evils until those who are really and truly philosophers acquire political power or until, through some divine dispensation, those who rule and have political authority in cities become real philosophers.*

– PLATO

Interestingly, Plato wrote this quote when he was in his seventies. As a young man, he had been a part of the social elite and was offered a guaranteed position in political power. However, upon examining the rulers of the day, he realized they were unjust and turned down this seemingly incredible offer and chose, instead, to study philosophy. As it turned out, the offered position of power was not guaranteed, and Plato made the right decision based upon his character. The "ruling 30," as they were called, were overruled and lost their power.

The Courage to stand up to sexist remarks

Do one thing every day that scares you.

– ELEANOR ROOSEVELT.

Sexism is an important area to address, and I have observed two extremes. On the one hand, women at times either "fly off the handle" at comments that do not deserve a strong reaction, or we passively dismiss and say nothing when truly damaging comments are made.

It is important here to learn to recognize the difference between the two extremes so that you can make change and still co-exist with your male counterparts. The other day, I was sitting with a businessman at a luncheon. He made a glib comment and out of the blue said, "All women are stupid," and then laughed. I immediately observed the nervous laughter of the woman sitting beside me and began to process his other behaviours, such as talking loudly on the phone during our conversation. So as Marcus Aurelius would state, "Shame on you if you expect something different when you know what you're dealing with." I observed that this man was uncouth in every way and so it should not surprise me that he would make such a remark. And I knew that if I countered him, he would not understand. So I proceeded to ensure that he would get my message loud and clear. I corrected him and asked him kindly not to make such statements in our company. He laughed and pressed for support from the gentleman I was with. Thank goodness this gentleman knew me well, for he said, "This is the last woman you should have said that to." This comment alone I consider to be a compliment that attested to the fact that I am known to speak up for anyone who is being slandered, regardless of gender or culture. The man who made the comment was counting on the other man to support him and for them to make light of the situation together so that he could save face. This did not happen, as I do not surround myself with men who support such comments.

This first choice of mine is crucial, for the people I surround myself with directly affect the language and interactions I have throughout the day. Adopting this strategy is one of the most important things you can do for yourself. Ensure that you can count on the people around you to support you. If you cannot, then you will want to reconsider whom you spend your time with, as your choice of peers can lead you into situations that may grow uncomfortable for you.

When the businessman realized he was losing ground, he reiterated "how stupid women are," and at this point I asked him to please respect that another gentleman was now talking and that his turn was over.

The situation was uncomfortable for him and I knew it, but I could not permit anyone to make such a blanket statement and continue to think that this attitude was acceptable to men or women. If people who make such comments want to spend time in my company, they must realize that it will not be comfortable for them, and I will not wear their toxicity. The power lies within me, not the comments of another.

I have had other men reveal their sexism over the years, and I will not do business with them if they do not demonstrate a capacity to respect the rights of people in their company, regardless of gender. Shutting these men out because of their comments about women is not the point. The reason I shut them out is not only to show them that I am *smarter* than their attitudes indicate, but also that I cannot count on them in a meeting to support the mandate of the mission when they do not respect my gender.

And so it stands to reason that if I do not respect my gender, then why should they? I believe this way, the ship begins to turn and we chart our course. By first respecting ourselves enough to demand treatment to keep our dignity intact, we are on our way to making real change.

Your Character is your best guide in decision making

Some philosophers believed there is almost a predestined track not unlike a rail system dictating the course of your life. If this track were destined to take everyone to a state of joy and a life of meaning, then all we need to know is how to stay on course.

The best mechanism for staying on our predetermined track is to rely on our character when faced with forks in the road. Character and doing what you know to be the right thing will always serve you.

And character is built by having a strong foundation in the virtues.

Victor Frankl, author of "Man's Search for Meaning," lived through the horrendous hardship of the concentration camps in Germany. There were many "so-called" opportunities to escape, but each one presented a compromise in Victor's character. As a result, he made decisions based upon his character and every time it was actually the best thing to do.

One example was the time they had a truck organized to smuggle several people living in the concentration camps out of the camp. Frankl was included in the plan and was to meet the group at a certain time after he'd finished his watch as a doctor in the medical building. However, his relief person did not show up and if he'd left, his escape would have been obvious and the people in his care would have suffered for his actions. So he chose to stay. You can imagine how upset he was that he'd missed his one chance out of hell and into perceived freedom. However, the truck was blown up as soon as it left the camp. Frankl realized he was saved and lived because he had followed his character. These kinds of incidents occurred frequently for Frankl, and it inspired him to share his theories on your character as your destiny with millions of others the world over. He called it Logotherapy.

Victor Frankl's philosophy of controlling one's attitude is another key element in leading a successful life. Even though he lost his wife and all his friends in the concentration camps, truly an unimaginable existence, he used that pain to create the world-famous Logotherapy. Millions of people the world over have his book and in it he uses his horrendous experience to show you that no one can take your joy from you. You have the power within yourself to find the joy you seek by following your character.

Logotherapy is used today for people who have gone through horrific experiences, from paralysis to losing a child. They must start to piece their lives together and the foundations are built upon finding their joy through the development of the virtues.

The most courageous act—a mother's love—Mercy's story

I think the most courageous thing a mother can do is part from her children temporarily or long-term to advance their lives. I marvel at women who are able to work away from their children to better the lives of their families. My only experience with this was during my journalism studies. My son was three years old and lived with his father for several months while I studied and worked full time Eventually he came back to live with me and I continued working and studying while taking care of my son by myself. That year taught me a great deal about myself and my will to advance my life and that of those around me.

Any North American working mother with children knows of nannies who come here to Canada, often from the Philippines, and who leave behind their young ones so they can care for our children. When I first heard of this, I was absolutely shocked that we could do this to other women. And then upon closer examination, I learned more about how this advances the lives of their families. I truly hope one day there will be a better way for women the world over to advance the lives of their children. I am not sure what we can do. If anyone has any suggestions on this, please let me know. I am serious about this. I am completely at a loss for how we can help educated mothers from other countries get their families to Canada more quickly.

My friend, Mercy, is a nanny here in North America. Jovilyn Mercy Culasing is 33 years old and a teacher by profession. She studied at a college in the Philippines and received her teaching diploma from Northern Luzon. She has three boys, ages three, seven and eight. She has not seen her boys for two years and will not see them for another year.

Mercy is the nanny for a very good friend of mine, and she and I have shed many tears talking about her children. Mercy is one of the most accommodating, helpful, intelligent and positive human beings I have ever come across. I knew interviewing Mercy would be insightful. I am always taken by people who demonstrate courage, particularly women to advance the lives of those around them. Mercy sleeps alone every night while her husband cares for their children thousands of miles away. The three year old doesn't really know Mercy, since he was just one when she left to build a better life for her family.

The children Mercy cares for have all the things you can dream of and Mercy gives them the most amazing, loving and selfless care, as she would her own children. Mercy once asked me if I had also enjoyed all the toys these children have growing up. She was surprised to learn that I went many Christmases without toys. She was surprised to learn that one in five children lives in poverty in North America. I was one of them. I think this was a real connection for us as I empathize with her desire to achieve prosperity for her children. My mother would have done anything in her power to give us a better life. I believe every mother would. Sometimes it just does not come together for one reason or another.

The Courage to leave to advance the lives of her children

Mercy was teaching in the Philippines for five years and then made the difficult decision to become a caregiver in North America because there is more opportunity here. And life in the Philippines is hard. "You earn just enough for one day. You are living day to day. There is no bright future," says Mercy. She is considered to be one of the lucky ones. There are many interviews and a lot of paperwork to come here. It took her two years to go through the process. Mercy chose short-term sacrifice over the eternity of no opportunity for her children.

"My husband is sad that I had to do this," she says. "But he could not stop this because he knows it is good for our family. I miss my children. I am strong because I have the determination to build a better future for my children. Faith in God gets me through. We have to hope in God that it will be a better life.

"Life for them now with my money is very big. I can send my children to private school. Before, they went to the public schools, which are crowded. But in private school they can learn English, which prepares them for Canada. Now they can buy what they want–food, clothes, the odd toy.

"My dream is to no longer be a caregiver. I want to study more so that I can become a care aid for seniors one day."

143

A mother's love

Mercy believes the love of a mother cannot compare to anything else. "The feeling that you can someday give them a better future is my driving force," says Mercy. "Better than what I was given as a child. I do not want them to ever experience what I did. I want them to be humble and have faith that they will have a better life."

A mother's courage

Mercy was a student of philosophy in college and draws from that knowledge to build ways to summon strength and courage. "I am being true to myself and I do not fear anything," she says. "I try my best to be honest all the time with myself. I have to be strong. I have the spirit to do this. I know I can do this. I know that this is not forever, that this is just for a short time and it is worth it. I would tell other women facing challenges not to give up and that you will get through."

I read Mercy's story and I am reminded of something Lisa said about living in Canada. Lisa really appreciates that, as a Canadian citizen she had the right to access higher learning so that she could advance her life and go from a high school dropout to Ph.D. I am also reminded that the poverty I had experienced was nothing compared to what Mercy experienced in the Philippines. It's all relative. We live in one of the greatest, if not the greatest, countries in the world, where a poor girl in a trailer in rural Nova Scotia can dream of going to university and owning her own business and make it her reality. You really just have to stop sometimes and feel incredibly grateful to live here. Every year I do my taxes and just before I want to complain, I reflect upon the health care and access to learning that we enjoy here compared to people the world over. I wish more people could have all this without the sacrifice Mercy has to go through. I wish more of us who are born here, would appreciate what we've been given by birthright.

And if Mercy can live three years of her life away from her children to advance their lives, I do not see how giving up one night a week to sit on Council or government committees to advance the lives of the people in our community, is some severe hardship for us as Canadian women.

Sometimes we just need perspective. The courage Mercy demonstrates should inspire all North American women to see that an evening or two a week is a small price to pay to advance society. Mercy would give anything to be away from her children for only one or two nights a week, instead of every day for three years straight.

VIRTUE

Justice

To achieve justice is the summit of success, since it is herein that failure most often occurs. Justice, itself, is not the exclusive responsibility of any one class of citizens, but emerges from the harmonious interrelationship of each component of the society with every other.

– MARCUS AURELIUS–THE MEDITATIONS

Never give in. Never, never, never, never in nothing great or small, large or petty, never give in except to convictions of honour and good sense. Never yield to force; never yield to apparently overwhelming might of the enemy.

– SIR WINSTON CHURCHILL

When you think of justice, what first comes to mind? For many of us we think of lawyers and court systems. And this would be correct, but it is not the whole picture. When there is a breakdown in justice, lawyers and courts are needed. But justice is the act of every citizen, each and every day, taking on the responsibility to do the right thing when faced with challenges or ethical dilemmas. And this pertains both to our personal lives and to our role as observers.

Justice is about understanding our place in our community, our country and our world. Once we understand our place of responsibility and do the things to move people toward right action, we are helping to build a just society.

Do you consider yourself to be a citizen? This is a very important question to ask of oneself.

Furthermore, do you consider yourself to be a *good* citizen? This is where we begin to demystify the ways of ensuring we live in a just society, by learning how to be involved and be active citizens so that we may live "The Good Life."

A citizen, according to the philosopher, Jean-Jacques Rousseau, is a person who is associated with a city.

So what does it mean to be associated with a city? At the most basic level, a person of legal age who votes could consider herself to be a citizen. An *active* and *involved* citizen is a person who goes further than the most basic right and responsibility of voting in elections. She works with other citizens, both men and women, as a collective to ensure their community is functioning in such a healthy way that *all* citizens are represented—every socio-economic group, every culture, gender, and age group.

There are so many injustices in the world. The ones I would like to address are those that we can do something about. And to get there, we return to the theme of the shift out of the patriarchal society, therefore addressing *real* issues behind poverty and how women can bridge the gap between rich and poor through the City. The model of economic development in the City has the power to bridge this gap and reveals some realistic ways for us to help shape the interrelation of healthy governments with business and non-profit.

We will also examine ways in which we can assist our young men to ensure they are learning co-operation and feeling a sense of belonging.

Terrorism—the extreme backlash from the shift out of the patriarchal society

All wars are fought for money.

– SOCRATES

When you look at the age we live in and the recent barrage of terrorist acts, you must know for certain that *none* of this is really because of loyalty to a "god," as stated by terrorists. First of all, terrorism is the most extreme symptom of the shift out of the patriarchal society. For centuries those men have enjoyed the subordination of women who were forced to cover their bodies and were not allowed to have the basic rights such as an education, clean drinking water and proper health care. But with the advancements in technology and in the age of Internet technology, women in these terrorist-controlled countries are becoming more aware of their rights and beginning to cast off their scarves and expect, and rightly so, the same rights as men.

Terrorists are simply into power and money. From the illegal drug and arms trades to the power they feel over women, this is all their war is about. This is a truly tragic injustice. And it has come upon our shores.

Do you consider yourself to be a global citizen?

This shows us that we are in a global world and in order to become a true global citizen, we must ensure we support our peacekeepers and direct and guide the ways in which we support the freedom of women and children. We must not be afraid, for fear is what gives evil people the power to continue to perform their injustices against women and children in the world.

We must do our homework and understand the issues in the world around us. War can seem so far away from our suburban worlds and suburban concerns. It was not until my best friend, Captain Trevor Greene, the bravest man I know, was severely injured by a man—someone who did not want to see the women and children in his village have free will—that I began to understand the situation in Afghanistan. The attacker broke the unwritten laws of the peaceful Shura in his village where Captain Greene sat without his helmet on as a show of respect to the elders. As he discussed ways to bring the basics of health care, clean drinking water and education and freedom with the village elders, this misguided adolescent brutally axed Trevor in the head. And although his people deserve the rights that are being fought for, they had been taught fear for so many centuries that none of them had the courage to intercept this barbaric act against Captain Trevor Greene.

From that day forward, March 4th, 2006, when my best friend was attacked, I have made the commitment to be brave in every daily situation. I will not stand for anyone being bullied in my presence. I use logic and right action, and although bullying in the workplace and the school yard in North America manifests itself differently than what Captain Greene and the people of Afghanistan experienced, we must make the commitment in our daily lives to follow right action and never allow anyone in our presence to suffer at the hands of a tormentor.

In the early days following the attack I would visit Trevor regularly in the hospital because we both lived in Vancouver. At that time, the paralysis made it difficult for him to even use his voice. But on occasion, in the early days, he was able to speak. On one such visit I found him looking reflectively out the window. I asked him what he was thinking and he said to me, "I want world peace."

Even now as he continues to work hard to regain movement in his body, he retains his core values. Trevor is truly a profound human being who believes firmly that we have an obligation to be fearless and do what it takes to ensure no woman, man or child is bullied.

Trevor's greatest gift is being the voice for those who cannot speak for themselves. He spent years in Japan and wrote a book on the homeless there. He advocated for the rights of the downtrodden. He wrote a book on the missing women in the Vancouver downtown east side. Forty-two women who worked in the sex trade were killed and it took years for the police to catch the killer. I still get e-mails from the women Trevor interviewed in the east side. One woman who worked in the sex trade wrote me to send Trevor her well wishes and for me to pass on to him that she got out of the sex trade because of a talk she had with him.

Trevor was not just a journalist who spoke on behalf of those who could not speak for themselves. He truly cared about and looked out for the rights of each and every person in his path. He is truly a philosophic person.

And now while Trevor works courageously to regain his mobility so that he can spend time with his fiancée and baby daughter, his friends are continuing his work to speak on behalf of those who cannot speak for themselves.

Utopia

I recently had to exercise this belief in never allowing anyone to be bullied in my own life. My son came home from his new middle school and was worried about a boy in his class. They were asked to write about their own Utopia and write down the things they did not want in their worlds. The boy beside him wrote that he did not want Jews in the world. Victor was shaken by this and wondered how someone could say such a thing in this day and age.

The following week Victor came home from school and this same boy had another bully slam Victor up against the lockers while this boy grabbed my son's jacket and tore it. Victor was reluctant to tell me about this incident, but because we talk every day, it came up and we discussed it.

The next day was a very busy day for me at work, but you can bet I cancelled appointments and took the time to take the jacket to the Principal and asked her to follow up on this. She was very attentive. I asked her to speak with the mother and the student and to ask the mother to have the jacket repaired so that she, herself, could have a talk with her son on his behaviour and explain to him that he has no right to lay a hand on another person, nor to cause fear in that person.

The Principal did just that and the mother agreed to repair the jacket. I am very proud of this boy's mother for she explained to her son that this was inappropriate and unacceptable behaviour. And he got it.

My son told me that this boy changed dramatically for the better because his family was engaged in the consequence and he fully understood he had to be accountable. He never bullied my son again. The reason we were fortunate is that my son had the courage to tell me what had happened, and the school staff were trained to assist both families. The family of the child who bullied was involved in the consequence.

Nasima's story

I have had the great honour to come to know Nasima Nastoh. She has taken the tragedy of the loss of her son and crusades to stop the bullying in schools. Nasima lost her son when he took his own life because he could no longer bear the bullying he endured in his school.

Nasima credits her very logical view of the world to her upbringing. She was raised in Afghanistan and her father was a poet and philosopher. He taught her about Plato and right action and the Good Society. He taught her that being a philosopher was something for both men and women and set about giving her the same education as her brothers.

Nasima to me, is the living embodiment of the power an individual has to see justice in new and profound ways. Nasima's philosophy is that you are either part of the problem or part of the solution. That's an interesting thing to check in on and ask ourselves, "Am I part of the problem or part of the solution?" And make the commitment to be part of the solution.

When Nasima's son, Hamed, committed suicide, he was in grade nine. Hamed was a strong student with top marks. One day he came home and wrote a five-page suicide letter to his family and then took his life because he found the taunting to be unbearable. None of us can imagine this, the highest level of pain: a mother losing her child.

Nasima was devastated, as any mother would be. She spent the following year in a deep depression. Her husband has still not gotten over Hamed's death and struggles with it.

Nasima then drew from her father's philosophical teachings. Nasima's father taught her that patience is a part of courage, that it is a kind of wisdom. She "stopped screaming at God" and straightened herself up and after a year of grieving, Nasima decided she was going to be a part of the solution.

In Hamed's letter, he asked his mother to go and tell others to stop the bullying. Members of her family told her to remain silent, for the shame of suicide was something they could not bear. Nasima mustered all the courage she could and got past the stigma of suicide and then began her mission to be the voice for Hamed.

At the time of Hamed's death, bullying was not widely understood in Canada. Nasima had no idea what it was until her son took his life as a result of it.

Now Nasima travels throughout western Canada, speaking at events and schools. There is never a dry eye in the house after she reads Hamed's suicide letter. It is a most profound presentation that moves everyone to check in with themselves to ensure they are a part of the solution.

"I did not know what bullying was," says Nasima. "And when I set out on this journey to break the silence and share with others the negative impacts of bullying, I began to get letters and phone calls from people all across the country of all ages. People writing to tell me that years after being bullied, they still carry the scars. Hamed wrote in his suicide letter telling me to go and tell everyone what bullying does to people and to motivate people to stop it. It was Hamed's one wish and I made a promise to myself and to Hamed that I will do everything I can to put a stop to this. There are serious consequences to bullying. When you look at the school shootings, these students who shoot other students were all bullied. So you can see the consequences go beyond the life of that child.

"I believe education is important—to enlighten youth on the consequences of bullying to themselves and the people around them. When I began this journey, my husband did not want me to speak with the media about suicide but I got past this shame because I want to save other children. I don't want other mothers to have to go through the pain of losing a child to bullying."

Live authentically

So many people are bound by social opinion. The *shame* of suicide was enough to keep most of Nasima's family in silence. Nasima's philosophical approach made saving the life of a child a bigger priority than what others may think of her. This is crucial when following right action to build a just society.

"The unbearable pain I suffered felt as if someone stuck a knife in my heart and at the time of his suicide, I wanted to die and be with Hamed. And then I realized that I could not bear for another mother to go through this. So when the media came to me and asked if Hamed was bullied, I said to myself, I don't care what people think, I have to help other mothers. What I am doing is for the safety of other children. Even if I save only one life, it's worth it. The most satisfying part of my talks are the letters I get from youth telling me that they had suicidal thoughts and that my talk of Hamed and showing them the pain of it made them choose to live. I have been stopped in stores by people who sat in the audience and they thank me for helping them see the hope in life."

If we ignore bullying, we send the message that it's OK

"We cannot ignore what is happening to our youth. Some people say, it's not my business, why should I talk about suicide? We have to get past the stigma and ask ourselves what can we do to prevent teen suicide?

"When I was a young child, my brother and I asked our father what does philosophy mean? And my father said, 'philo' means love and 'sophia' means wisdom. That philosophy is a love of wisdom. My father did not care for material things; his love was for wisdom, leading and right action. He taught us that patience is a kind of wisdom."

Nasima's talks promote respect for each other and peace. She went on to form the Safe School Task Force that makes bullying a subject that is understood by teachers and students alike as intolerable. Nasima is a well put-together, confident woman who lights up the room when she speaks. She wants other women to know that it was not always this way. The year after Hamed's death had her crying at the "drop of a hat" and feeling a real sense of hopelessness. But when she began to draw from her philosophical education and spoke with her father, he reminded her that there is patience in courage and there is a wisdom in being patient. She could not bring Hamed back, but she could save other children.

"My life was falling to pieces and I decided to pick up my pieces and realized I could move forward, because I wanted to make a difference. I did not want Hamed's death to be in vain. I wanted to find some value in this for others so that Hamed's life would have renewed meaning and purpose. I realized that one person *can* make a difference.

"When I embarked on this journey, I was the first person who was really saying that bullying has got to stop and bringing it to the forefront. I spoke with Mayors, I spoke with MLAs, I spoke with MPs. We formed the Safe School Task Force in 2001 because of Hamed. I have been in front of the Legislature twice to change the legislation so that bullying would be classed as a criminal offence. The deterrent of being charged for bullying would help prevent this kind of act.

"Children learn by example. Adults have a responsibility not to bully others themselves. Bullying is a long-standing problem. When I talk at the schools, my main point is that we have to celebrate our differences. We must accept those who are not like us. Some kids do not even know that what they are doing is wrong, perhaps because someone is bullying them at home. When someone bullies, they are more than likely being hurt by someone else. So we need to look at this and the root of the problem and our own behaviours as adults and parents and caregivers and in what we teach our children through our own actions and what we say about others in the home.

"We have had bullies watch the video on Hamed's suicide letter. I have had these former bullies come up and hug me because they did not know how much pain they had caused. They did not know they were hurting others. They made the commitment to change their ways. It is so important to know yourself. We must teach our children awareness. Violence does not solve anything. People who act violently do not love themselves."

Nasima's words for other women

Nasima acknowledged there are many challenges facing women, and from her experience she wanted others to find that value in the tragedy to move forward. "Don't stop moving forward. Listen to your gut," says Nasima. "Trust your inner voice. You can overcome anything. It is important to maintain a positive attitude. And most importantly, allow yourself to be yourself. Learn to be your true self. I always say there's a reason an original piece of art is worth more than a copy. So be your own work of art, not an imitation, but an authentic original."

Hamed, Nasima's son, was bullied for being himself. And yet Nasima champions the importance of being authentic, and is spreading the message to other youth to allow peers to be themselves. When someone bullies another for being different, it is sending the message that it is not OK to be yourself. That is why Nasima gives her talks to youth to ensure that everyone understands that it is more than OK to be your authentic self. And it's important for us, as women, to do the work in our own lives to find our authentic voice so that we can show our children, through our actions and words, that being yourself is most important in living and leading.

Nasima's message to women is that you are very strong. "Women are very strong. The root to this strength is to find the good in every situation, to be positive. I have a very challenging life and the reason why I am successful in my work, in my mission is because I have a positive attitude in the face of these challenges. This allows me to find the good. Get rid of all doubts and have faith in yourself. Life is not a straight line. We must be open to changes and adapt when the world changes around us," says Nasima.

This is a reminder that the practice of the virtues strengthens them. Nasima chose to practice courage rather than self-pity. It was when she made the conscious decision to be courageous and go against the fear of being stigmatized for her son's suicide, that the leader within her emerged. Her focus of helping others in fact helped her to come out of the pain she was living in over the loss of her son. It is when we see our role in the bigger picture of society, we begin to lead *The good life*. Nasima's talks have prevented countless potential acts of violence by giving bullies clear perspective on the consequences of their actions.

Find your strengths

Nasima works with teachers and police officers on the subject of bullying, not just in the classrooms and on the street but with their own children. She often asks these adults to reflect upon what their strengths and talents are. "Once I asked a teacher who was concerned about her teenager to share with me her strengths. She looked at me and said she did not have any. And I told her that the fact she called me to talk about her child, is a strength. We often undervalue what our strengths are."

Bullying is negative energy

I remember reading *Lord of the Flies* in high school. I will never forget the message that the "pack mentality" can be brutal in the bullying of another. I will never forget Piggy and how everyone attacked him.

It's interesting to note that even in our workplace, there is bullying. People form groups and have likes and dislikes for certain people. I have seen bullying in Council chambers and in committee meetings. I have been bullied in committee meetings and was even told on one occasion that when I speak up, certain male committee members see me as what Barbara Bush referred to as something that rhymes with *witch*. I have stood my ground and made no apologies for working towards right action in the face of inferior people seeking power through bullying. I even had a very weak mayor threaten to have my job if I continued to write my column. Needless to say, I continued to write the column.

I have prevailed in these cases and have learned first-hand not to be afraid. I am guided by the belief that I have a certain level of expertise and understanding which has earned me the right to give talks as an expert on economic development, from the World Urban Forum to the BC Tourism Conference. I will never apologize for seeing the gap between rich and poor and providing sound, just solutions that ensure everyone is included.

An aquaintance once said to me, "Most women are not like you, we don't do the things you do." My immediate response to her was, "I am no different, after each time I seek justice or press further, I go home, check in with myself, reassure myself that this is the right direction and start all over the next day."

The reason other women and I are able to work through these challenges, as we shift out of the patriarchal society, is that I take the high road and never strip the other person of their dignity, regardless of their behaviour. At the same time, I will not hesitate to use logic and the strength of my argument to reveal their hidden agendas for power. That is my commitment and obligation to the people who are counting on me to speak the truth in the pursuit of justice. Whether I am revitalizing neighbourhoods with a goal to ensure that a single mom can feel safe enough to buy milk at night in our commercial areas or when I am speaking out on bullying in my column, nothing scares me, not even threats because I have taken this risk and broken through to see that nothing good comes when good people do nothing. We must have the collective courage to make change for the greater good.

I do not get stuck on why someone has bullied me. I do not breathe life into it or give it any of my attention. My attention is focused upon my work, right action and serving the people who are counting on me. The people I serve do not need me to get broken up about someone's comments. They are counting on me to walk through this. I think, as adults we should have the strength and philosophical virtues to do this. Our youth are far more senstive to this kind of behaviour, for they are just forming their sense of the world around them. They need us to be examples of the virtues in action so they may learn how to walk through the challenges of life and feel empowered to be a part of the solution rather than the problem.

This is where the Socratic Method comes in for us when facing illogical opposition with hidden agendas. We must use reason over emotion in countering all kinds of challenges in our work. As Nasima reminds us, if we can remain positive during the challenges we face, we are halfway there.

The health of the individual and the health of the city

Now we'll examine how Plato applied the virtues to the lives of individual human beings and the parallel between the citizen and the city.

What do people's weight issues have to do with the decay of the City?

Everything!

You will see that the condition of being overweight resembles a state of urban decay. Both show a disconnection—between the parts of the soul of the individual in the case of a physical weight issue, and between the three levels of the city when there is urban decay.

The biggest challenge facing the health of the individual in North America is obesity.

The biggest challenge facing the health of the city is urban decay.

Can they be fixed?

Both of these issues can be reversed through the application of philosophy. We addressed the weight issue in the chapter on **Moderation** and now we will address the issue of urban decay in this chapter through the model of economic development.

In Plato's *Republic*, the philosopher drew an analogy between the running of the city, or society, and the individual life of a citizen. Plato surmised that both the city and the citizen share the same virtues, and that the citizen is not unlike the city in the way it performs actions and embodies the virtues. Hence the challenges of running a city are not unlike the challenges of running our own daily lives; that when pulled in different directions, with no firm sense of the virtues, both the citizen and the city can make unhealthy choices. These unhealthy choices are reflected in our individual weight issues and the urban decay we are seeing in our cities.

And Plato's analogy gets really interesting in terms of how we can learn from philosophy and apply it to our real everyday quest for a just society with the analogy of the soul.

Plato believed that you can draw a parallel between the land, buildings and resources of the city and the human body of the citizen. The soul, he said, has three parts that can be compared to the three classes of citizens that need to contribute to make the city function in a healthy way.

So if you think about the following three parts of your soul, as laid out by Plato, you can see how a balance among the three is essential to leading a healthy life.

The Rational Soul—which is the intellect (virtue of **wisdom**): This is the part of us that makes wise judgements and can drill down to determine what is real and true so that we live the healthiest life possible by making rational decisions.

The Spirited Soul—which is our will (virtue of **courage**): This is the part that acts out what the mind has judged to be the best course of action. This is where we courageously follow through on what we have decided we should do in situations.

The Appetitive Soul—which is desire (virtue of **moderation**): This is our emotional part, the part of us that wants instant gratification. Often we resist these desires and opt to follow moderation so that we can have other, longer-term benefits in our lives.

In Plato's view, a human being is healthy when all three parts of the soul are working in harmony for the good of the person as a whole. The parallel is drawn to a city which demonstrates the same kind of harmony among its three groups of citizens—all working together for the good of the whole city.

Rational Soul
Wisdom

Spirited Soul
Courage

Appetitive Soul
Moderation

As in a well-organized state, the justice of an individual human being emerges only from the interrelationship among its separate components.

– PLATO

And for this to really make sense in our every day lives, Plato's theory of our nature, as human beings, gives us the answer to the question of why justice is preferred over injustice. If you were to follow the three-part soul theory, you would see that true justice can be likened to good health, which we can only achieve through the harmony of the three parts of our soul. We are being unjust to ourselves, as individuals when we allow ourselves to lead a life with our souls in disarray. And the unhealthy city is being unjust to itself with the three groups of people merely co-existing with each other and, therefore functioning, poorly. You have to achieve harmony and balance and this can only be achieved when all citizens are represented in the city, or in the case of the individual, when all parts of the soul are balanced.

And harmony of the city state *requires* that women be in positions on Council as well as management in the administration. For it is women's gift for collaboration that will ensure we build and foster the model of economic development which will reverse the biggest challenge of the city state today—urban decay.

The model of economic development

But one power should not be thrown down to exalt another—for all power intoxicates weak man; and its abuse proves, that the more equality there is established among men (and women), the more virtue and happiness will reign in society.

– MARY WOLLSTONECRAFT

When we are in a competitive state and do now allow room for equal representation among men and women, we will continue to have societal ills such as urban decay and poverty.

Through the course of my career, I have had the great honour to work with a diverse range of men and women. One particular contract allowed me to work under a female Mayor and senior female managers. This collaboration with wise male and female members of the team allowed us to build a model of economic development that would reverse urban decay. This is still no easy feat, but I will share our experience with you.

When I began working on a contract dealing primarily with tourism, I began to see the important link between tourism and the commercial areas. For when a visitor comes to our town, they want to feel safe and welcomed to an environment that provides a sense of place and a good experience that they will tell others about. When we began, there were three key areas experiencing urban decay and the business owners wanted to do something about it. My first thoughts were always about the single mom and her safety when needing to go out at night to pick up milk at the corner store for her children. I saw her as clear as day, and wanted to ensure we created a commercial area where she could safely do this.

We began to see the commercial areas were becoming more crime-ridden with issues around break-ins, prostitution, graffiti and overall decay. The population was increasing rapidly, expected to double in size in 15 years, and if not dealt with properly, was in danger of spiraling to an unmanageable level. So my female manager and female

Mayor listened to my recommendation and established that these "pressure points" as I referred to them—those areas sensitive to sliding into serious problems—would get priority and we would facilitate revitalization task forces to bring all partners to the table and leave no one out.

This is exactly what Jean-Jacques Rousseau and Mary Wollstonecraft advocate in their great philosophical works.

The Pilot Project—Maillardville

The Pilot Project of Maillardville is where we begin. This community in British Columbia had the highest percentage of single moms in our city, one of the lowest levels of education, and was beginning to show some serious signs of urban decay. The bus shelters had the windows smashed out, the seats were gone, graffiti was everywhere, and so it went on down the street. So where do you begin?

You begin with a theme that brings everyone together

Once you find an authentic, grass-roots theme that everyone from the wealthy developers to the social services team can believe in, you are well on your way to making change. That theme is your hook to ensure that everyone can see the same vision, regardless of what direction they are coming from. For Maillardville, we recognized its rich Francophone heritage and culture. It was the oldest and largest Francophone community in British Columbia, and so we set about leveraging that theme and its connection to the 2010 Olympic and Paralympic Games. We recognized that the Olympic Games shared the same two official languages as Canada—English and French—and when the world comes for the Olympic Games, they would expect an authentic Francophone experience. This was an important connection for us, as it brought in new government funding which we could leverage. Because the Federal and Provincial governments and the city showed their commitment to rebuilding the community, partners were attracted to sit at our table and work together.

Everyone shared vision of a vibrant French-themed commercial area. This vision was enough to bring diverse stakeholders together to work to clean up the area and attract new investment so that the vision would come to life.

See the gold in everything

It is important to note that we focused on the good: the rich heritage, the vibrant community spirit, the festivals, and seeing the Olympic Games as a catalyst for change. We began to visualize the future together and began to have regular monthly meetings. The task force included everyone: developers, heritage and culture organizations, Francophone groups, social services professionals, seniors, the arts community, festival planners, the residents' association, business improvement groups, city staff, and Council chairs.

With three levels of government, non-profit and private sector working together, we had liftoff. The area was beautified using a French theme with façade architectural strategy. Flowers lined the streets, and the bus shelters were cleaned up. We began to hold festivals in the streets, organize clean-up days, and distribute neighbourhood newsletters and we created a residents association that worked with the business improvement group. People were no longer isolated, but connected to each other. They were better using their resources as a collective.

We then began to work with the local university to work towards bringing the Humanities 101 project to our community to ensure that anyone living below poverty or in the street who never had access to higher education would have the opportunity to study philosophy and the humanities. In other major cities this program has enabled people living in poverty to recognize that they have all the resources available to them to lead the greatest life possible, and that it is just a matter of identifying those resources through a new way of thinking.

And the same can be said of our economic development model which had in the past been focused only on attracting business; now it was not only about attracting business but how those businesses would enhance the lives of the residents, and vice versa.

This enlightened approach was applauded, and the Maillardville revitalization project was chosen to represent our province at the World Urban Forum in 2006. Our revitalization model both acknowledged that urban decay will be the biggest issue facing the cities of North America in the next 10–15 years while offering a pro-active, philosophy-based solution. This window in time is a crucial moment for us to shift our thinking in every city to ensure that we are engaging our citizens to live boldly and creatively in reversing urban decay. The reversal of urban decay is dependant upon the healthy city state that involves all people in the city to work together.

The philosopher, Socrates felt that it was just as important for women to give birth to ideas as it is to give birth to children. This is an important shift for us, as women, to know that our ideas are just as important as having children. If we could begin to value our ideas and have faith in our creativity to reverse societal ills, then we will narrow the gap between rich and poor.

In the revitalization effort of the Francophone community, we worked with staff to trademark the "Flaunt your Frenchness™" campaign which invited everyone to embrace whatever it is that they love about the French culture. It went on to win two national marketing awards from the Economic Developers Association of Canada. In its third year we used the campaign to launch a new branding strategy for the neighbourhood and began to work with Francophone businesses in Quebec to start our expansion and revitalization strategy. We attracted developers who shared the French vision but who also had a social vision. One such company was VanCity Enterprises, who bought land and began to work with our Task Force to shape development that would take in the needs of the community.

We gave birth to some fun ideas which allowed us to communicate who we are and where we're going. These ideas were trademarked, protected, and nurtured, but they also had deeper underlying goals such as supporting the single mom and ensuring that we looked out for our children. The beautification of the area allowed the residents to see themselves differently, in new and positive ways, with everyone having a seat at the table when making change.

Wisdom

VI

The more extensive a man's knowledge of what has been done, the greater will be his power of knowing what to do.

– BENJAMIN DISRAELI

The further back you look, the further ahead you will see.

– WINSTON CHURCHILL

The most important way to obtain wisdom is to have a strong sense of history. Marcus Aurelius said it did not matter whether it's 40 years or 40,000 years, mankind is doomed to make the same mistakes unless we learn the lessons from the past.

This is another very important reason to read the great philosophers of the past. They were often leaders in times of war and strife. It is interesting to note that when we examine the healthy model of economic development, it has its roots in *The Social Contract*, written by Jean-Jacques Rousseau over 200 years ago. Again, this shows us that nothing changes, just how our issues manifest themselves. As Churchill said, "The further back you look, the further ahead you will see."

We must, in all our infinite wisdom, begin to take advantage of the great teachings and wisdom of the past philosophers so that we may advance in this lifetime. We must let go of this notion that our small window in time is so important. We are no more important than the people who walked these very same streets 100 years ago, and we are no more important than those who will walk our streets 100 years from now. All we can do is ensure that we leave this earth a better place than we found it. And then we die. That is our reality. So each and every day we are on this earth, we have great opportunities to stretch ourselves and ensure the world around us is enhanced.

It is so interesting when you get into philosophical discussions with people about life and the meaning of life. Recently I heard two senior managers on separate occasions express serious concern about what will be written on their gravestones or what people will say about them at their funerals. Wow! We really have missed the boat if this is what we think is important. As Marcus Aurelius would tell you, no one is going to remember you. Even those who speak at your funeral will die, too, one day, and no one will remember them. So the reality is to forget yourself completely and go fearlessly into living a great life and leaving this world a better place than when you entered it. That is all there is. But should you do this willingly and care only for the fearless good work you must do, you will live with greatness and an inner light that will make every moment on this earth for you the most enjoyable one. And isn't that really all there is?

So while we are here, it's crucial that we give birth to beautiful ideas and know we have all the resources available to us to make these beautiful ideas our reality. It begins with visualization.

No question about it—I have visualized everything I have today, from my experience as an entrepreneur to where I live, to the people I surround myself with. I am blessed with two wonderful children, a partner that I love and respect, close friends and work that excites me.

It wasn't always this way. I didn't always have the life I wanted. In fact, my early years were quite the opposite. I was raised by a single mom and my sister and I took on jobs to feed our family. This is not something I used to share with too many people, but now I feel that it's important for me today to be a real life example of the power of visualization.

Here are the ten steps to visualization that I give to youth

First Step: Keep your eye on your goal—see it, visualize it, and it will happen.

Your body's nervous system doesn't know the difference between reality and imagination. This would explain why people who are told they can accomplish great things do, and those who are told they cannot, are not as likely to accomplish their goals. There was a book written called "Psycho-cybernetics" that was written by Maxwell Maltz about the power of visualization. This book teaches you how to visualize.

And you can put yourself on a training program for visualization like a workout program.

Every day for 28 days you do a visualization exercise and over time it becomes a daily practice naturally. So for 28 days take just 30 minutes and sit in a quiet area and visualize your life. See it as if you are watching a movie of yourself. See the size you are, the clothes you are wearing, the things you are doing, the work or job you are in, the people that you surround yourself with. Do this and you will begin to make these ideas your reality.

When I was eight years old, I visualized myself as a grown woman in a power suit doing good things for my community. It really didn't matter that we had no socks in the winter and often went to school without lunch. Our family had fallen on hard financial times, and yet my mother told me I could be and do anything I chose. My sister and I lived by this message and held fast to it. My sister has her Ph.D in Virology and is working on a vaccine for a Biotech company. And I have two degrees and a diploma. Nothing stopped either of us from reaching our goals.

Second Step: Know there are only two things that can stop you from realizing your dreams. *The first is fear and the second is you.* Only you and any fears you have will prevent you from living a happy and successful life. No one else will ever be to blame. Not your parents, not your teachers, not your lack of income, not your lack of access to things. Just yourself.

Now here's where visualization gets complex:

Third Step: In order to visualize long-term success, you need to see how every day presents opportunities to get you to your next goal.

After my degree in Sociology, I realized I wanted to travel. I had been to Mexico and Chicago and wanted to get involved in the travel industry. I got my diploma in Travel and Tourism and took some business courses at Dalhousie University, in Halifax, Nova Scotia. I got a job as a flight attendant and was so excited when I got a stack of tickets to anywhere in the world.

At first we worked to travel—you can bet I've been to New York,

Toronto, Scotland, Hawaii and have been coast-to-coast in Canada. I also loved pouring coffee!!! Yes, I looked forward to work every day. I considered my aircraft to be a "flying boardroom." I was in a position to speak with executives who I would never otherwise meet on the ground. I met former Canadian Prime Minister, Pierre Trudeau, author and media host Michael Harris, who told me I could write a book, and my mentor, Merv Russell, who owned 28 radio stations in Atlantic Canada who told me I could run my own company. I was so happy to learn from these people and share my ideas that I began to work with the marketing department of our airline and eventually started my own radio show.

Now I had no choice but to work at the airline, as I was putting my former husband through university. The pay was below poverty, and yet I enjoyed every minute of it. So it's crucial that you find the joy and do the learning you need, to advance yourself no matter *where* you are in your journey. There was a time when I could not leave my job, as I had fallen in love with one of the nicest men in the world. He also happened to be a high school drop-out with a dream: he wanted to be an engineer and live in British Columbia. You guessed it, my ex-husband is now a senior engineer and he lives in BC. Which leads me to my next step—instead of seeing my job as an interim one, I saw it as far more, as a stepping stone filled with opportunity. The philosophers would have you realize that regardless of the circumstances, there are enough resources available to you if you choose to see them. Many of the flight attendants saw only the juice boxes, trolleys and tickets, but did not see the people and the network these people could provide and as a result, they missed out on the possibilities that surrounded them.

Fourth Step: Share your dreams with others. My former husband told me that he wanted to be an engineer. I recognized that he was bright and just hadn't been blessed with the kinds of people whose support I enjoyed. So I supported him. It took seven years to get his degree and during that whole time, I flew around in my "flying boardroom."

Now I don't recommend putting someone through school to everyone. We had our challenges. But do tell people your dreams. Adults who worked hard to be where they are, will naturally want to share that wisdom with you. It does not matter how old you are, share your dreams with others, and they will help you to make it a reality.

Fifth Step: Find mentors. Seek out and surround yourself with people who can help you realize your dreams. Tell these people what you would like to do. People, especially adults who have accomplished things of substance in their lifetime, want to help. How do you find these people? They are sitting beside you, they are your teachers, principals, vice-principals, guidance counselors, your boss at your part-time job, your family, and you can seek them out. There are mentors everywhere—they can happen organically by connecting with someone whom you admire, or there are programs available. The Rotary Club is the perfect place to start.

When I was doing my undergraduate degree, I wanted to travel to the third world and volunteer. I applied to a program called Canada World Youth, and I was accepted. Now, my friends and family discouraged me from interrupting my studies, so I declined. I then met a girl who continued her studies in another country through a Rotary Scholarship. I didn't have access to Rotary when I was young, but vowed I would tell every student about this program and to apply for it. If you volunteer and have an interest as a global citizen, you may just earn a $20,000 Ambassadorial scholarship from your local Rotary Club. Contact them to learn more about this amazing opportunity.

Sixth Step: Get an Education. Go to university or college—take courses that will give you the skills to get to the next step. When I was in grade 11, I wanted to go to King's College to study the Foundation Year Program. It was widely known as the foundation of great philosophies that you could build your education upon. There was just one problem: back in 1986 we didn't have the Internet and my guidance counselor told me he didn't have any applications to this program. So I jumped on a bus and traveled the two hours to get the application. I got in. Now, getting to school with no money was going to be a bit of a challenge. So I took out a student loan, jumped back on the bus with five dollars in my pocket, and landed at King's College. My roommate lent me sheets for my bed, and I went on to become the co-president of the King's College BC Alumni Chapter. *Imagine if I'd ever thought money was an issue.*

Seventh Step: Observe the people who inspire you—take note of the people and their experiences that inspire you. When I was doing my undergraduate degree in Sociology, I worked as an after-school teacher at a local pre-school. I recall one day when a mother in her mid-thirties came in to pick up her child. She was ecstatic that she had paid off her student loan. I recall her great joy and what a feeling that must have been.

When I turned 34 I finally paid off student loans for two degrees and a diploma. It took many years. It was a feeling of accomplishment and freedom that I visualized all those years ago. Which leads me to my next step.

Eighth Step: Treat everyone with the same amount of respect. The greatest leaders treat everyone with the same level of respect. When I was a flight attendant, I noticed that the most successful CEOs treated everyone the same. Whether you were pouring coffee, handling baggage or seated beside them in business class, the greatest leaders treated everyone the same. I recall one day speaking with a CEO who was traveling with his little boy. His son was tired so I immediately got him a blanket and pillow and closed the window blind so he could rest. I thought nothing of it. Then his father stopped me and shared with me that he, himself, was, as he put it, "the most difficult person to please" and that he had written a letter of praise about me to the airline. He said, "I am going to tell you why I am writing this letter for you. You treated my son with the same respect you showed everyone else on this plane." All I could think of was how nice, and yet, how could anyone *not* treat everyone the same?

He then went on to ask me what I *really* wanted to do. He could see that I was a professional who could engage in conversation and felt I should be doing bigger things. I told him not to worry, that I was studying and had plans, but that the most important thing for me to do that day, at that moment in time, was to **serve.** I told him I was no different than he was. As a CEO, he was serving his company and employees and clients. He agreed with me. I will never forget that conversation. Which leads me to my next step. CEOs and leaders were often "nerds."

I had no idea that I was a nerd in high school. In fact, I thought I was pretty cool. It wasn't until I returned home for a wedding that I was told otherwise. I went home to Antigonish, Nova Scotia, for a dear friend's wedding and realized that I didn't know half of the "cool" people at the wedding. I spoke with the bride, and asked her why I didn't know half of the people there. She looked at me and said, "Barb, you were a nerd!" We had the greatest laugh.

I guess I was a "nerd." I had a job, I volunteered, I was in the high school play and I wrote for the school newspaper. I was too busy getting involved with activities with other "nerds" that I never got to know the cool people who were busy hanging out.

Ninth Step: The revenge of the "nerds" is success. There was a movie when I was young called "Revenge of the Nerds."

Now this is obviously not about revenge. But it's an interesting take on what really does happen as you grow up. One of the things I began to notice very quickly in my younger years was that at the end of an event or function, I was usually sitting with the CEOs and other leaders of groups. This continues to happen to me today. In fact, more often than not, I am enjoying the conversation of a CEO or political leader and learning something.

And it's pretty safe to say they were not part of what was the "cool crowd" in high school either. In fact, my business mentor in British Columbia introduced himself to me as a "nerd." I looked right back at him and said, "me too!!!"

Tenth Step: Never stop being a student and a teacher. In order to be successful, you must continue to learn every day of your life.

As you advance, you will find that you become the teacher in some instances and in others, you will be the student. It would be dangerous to assume that you know everything at any point in your life. Work towards becoming an expert at what you love. But never close your mind to learning more and advancing in wisdom.

You have the ability and power within you to be whatever you need to do to be happy and successful in your life. I know this from my own experience. When I was eight years old, I envisioned myself as I am today. It didn't matter that, as a child, my family lived in a remote town in Nova Scotia. It didn't matter that we sometimes went without socks in the wintertime. It never mattered that we fell on hard times financially. The reason it didn't matter was because I believed that I had the ability and power to do whatever I needed to do to be happy and successful. I saw the resources all around me. I saw all the golden opportunities in the seemingly mundane. I saw the power of mentorship beyond the trolley and juice boxes at the airline, I saw the beautiful work of art hiding beneath all that weight in my youth, and now I see the vibrancy of a community beyond the urban decay.

The road to visualizing your future is never going to be a simple one—it wasn't a straight line for me from being an eight-year-old with a vision of doing good things in the community through business. It was, and continues to be, a zig-zag path. There were many times when I stood back as if I was at a crossroads without a compass—unsure of the next step to take. That is to be an expected part of your journey.

This is the message I share with high school youth at conferences. At the end I always share what it takes to be happy. These are the things that can make a person happy—it's a formula that cannot fail. And as unique as each of us is, this formula is universal and applies to everyone.

Memorize the four things that bring happiness

1. Make sure you have strong and meaningful relationships with friends, family and peers. Ensure the people who surround you support you, and are a positive and reassuring part of your life.

2. Ensure that you find the work or studies that you love. Do not waste a moment of your life not seeing the value in your present day and where you are at—and if you find that your work compromises your ethics in any way—move on. Never compromise your values or ethics in anything you do.

3. Volunteer. Volunteering is the greatest way to selflessness; it is the key to overcoming fears and gaining wisdom. Fear happens when we are overly conscious of ourselves. Volunteering is the fastest way to forget yourself and to forget your ego and to think about others—I have volunteered for 20 years and credit a great

deal of my success to giving of my time to others. It comes back in the most unexpected ways, usually in the form of instant joy, and later on in wisdom.

4. Take nothing personally. Let go of your desire to take things personally. Let go of your ego and walk through challenges with a precision focus on your work at hand. When we realize we are just one part of the solution and that we are not so important, then we are able to really live greatly and get good things done.

Now you might be wondering, what do nice clothes do for a person, or a leather couch, or a new car. These are *pleasures*—and yes, we should all be able to enjoy the pleasures and rewards of our work, but they will never, ever make you *happy*. I enjoy shopping as much as the next person, but I recognize that it is a pleasure to shop. Happiness can only come from our relationships with our work, people, and from volunteering. Keeping them straight will give your life greater meaning. It is important to know the difference between what will bring you happiness and what will bring you pleasure.

And lastly, if you remember one thing, it's my final formula. The most simple formula to guaranteed successful living and joy is: *85 per cent attitude and 15 per cent skill.*

Your attitude in any situation will carry you much further than any amount of education degree or wealth. A positive attitude shown towards everyone you meet will be your anchor to success.

On having a personal mission statement

If a man's life has no consistent and uniform aim, it cannot itself remain consistent and uniform.....Accordingly, the aim we should propose for ourselves must be the benefit of our fellows and the community. Whosoever directs his every effort to this will be imparting uniformity to all his actions, and so will achieve consistency with himself.

– MARCUS AURELIUS

I cannot overemphasize the importance of having a personal mission statement. This statement alone will guide you through the most incredible of challenges. It's interesting when you talk with people and ask how many have a personal mission statement to find out that most don't. It is a rare occurrence to meet someone who has defined their mission statement and lives by it like a guiding light or force.

I did not realize I had a mission statement until someone pointed it out to me. Several years ago, I was at an Economic Development Conference in Victoria, BC. I was chatting with Colleen Rohde, the Economic Development Officer for Port Moody, BC. I was telling her how I wish to have the Wisdom of Solomon by the time I am 96. She looked at me and pointed out that this is a mission statement and that everyone should have one. You would not have a business without a mission statement; it would therefore stand to reason that you would not run your life without a guiding mission.

As a child I was fascinated by the story of King Solomon. I used to carry around a record and play it for anyone who would listen. I gave it to my teachers to play for the class. You may recall the story where the two women reported to Solomon because they are fighting over a baby. One woman claimed that the other woman stole her baby and left a dead baby instead. The two are fighting and both are claiming to own the child. King Solomon had to make a decision and announced that he would simply cut the child in half. Of course he never intended to do this, but it was his way of watching for a reaction from the women to provide him with clues as to who was the true mother of the child. One woman said, "Go ahead, cut the baby in half." The other mother said, "No, spare the child, let her have it."

King Solomon gave the baby to the woman who asked that it be spared, as he could see this was the voice of a woman who obviously loved the child like a true mother.

I am fascinated by the process of thinking with wisdom and following right action. With this mission statement as my guiding force, it also ensures that I am brought into the company of people of wisdom. My mentors, friends, and my Rotary Club are all people of wisdom. I am drawn to these people because my mission is to obtain the wisdom of Solomon by the time I am 96.

This mission statement causes me to learn, read, and study all the time. This mission means I want to learn constantly. It allows me to take risks. My risks are well-researched with a small margin for error. But this means I will still make mistakes as I am learning and seeking more wisdom.

Often small mistakes are wonderful, as they prepare you for something that could have been catastrophic later on down the road. But with the lesson in the earlier mistake, you are prepared for the big incident that you may face later on. Recall Winston Churchill and the battle early on that caused the loss of a lot of men. As tragic as this was, it was the lesson they needed in order to win the war.

The mission statement I follow also ensures that I stay on track. If you know where you are going, then no one can manipulate you or push you with their agenda.

My earlier mentor told me that people will have agendas for you, particularly when you are young. It is crucial that you stay on your track and a mission statement will keep you on that path.

When I am 96 and life presents an incredible challenge to me and I am left to sift through and find the truth, and then implement it with courage and conviction, I want to see that I have been a part of making justice in the lives of others.

Marcus Aurelius

The Meditations, which Marcus Aurelius wrote in 121 A.D. has stood the test of time and rests on the bedside table of many great leaders and many presidents, including former President, Bill Clinton. And so this book, intended for a male audience just as Mary Wollstonecraft had asserted that Rousseau had done with the Social Contract, I offer as a perfect guide for both men and women.

In book eight Marcus Aurelius wrote:

> *It will tend to avert complacency if you remember that any claim to have lived as a philosopher all your life, or even since reaching manhood, is now out of the question: indeed, it is as evident to many others as it is to yourself that even today philosophy is still*

far beyond you. Consequently your mind remains in a state of confusion as it grows no easier to earn the title of philosopher; also, your station in life militates constantly against it.

Once all this is seen in its true light, you should banish any thoughts of how you may appear to others, and rest content if you can make the remainder of your life what nature would have it to be.

Learn to understand her will, and let nothing else distract you.

Up to now, all your wanderings in search of the good life have been unsuccessful; it was not to be found in the casuistries of anything else. Where, then, lies the secret?

In doing what man's nature seeks. How so? By adopting strict principles for the regulation of impulse and action. Such as? Principles regarding what is good or bad for us: thus, for example, that nothing can be good for man unless it helps to make him just, self-disciplined, courageous, and independent; and nothing bad unless it has the contrary effect.

- MARCUS AURELIUS

Work to your talents!

Often a phrase or word message will pop up in my mind like a neon sign. I can see the word phrase as if I am reading it. The phrase, "work to your talents," has become a conscious mantra that I repeat over and over to myself daily, now without even trying. Say it to yourself right now, three times. The repetition of this phrase is what makes working to my talents a steady and consistent message keeping me focused and on track.

So often we are evaluated at work or by our peers. Often the focus is on what your weaknesses are and what you need to improve upon. There is no way that focusing on what you "can't do" will ever strengthen you. There is no reason that you have to be all things to all people. What if you could just focus upon your talents and strengths and work to them? Your work would improve and your relationships would flourish.

And many coaches and philosophers will focus on feedback from others. This can be a double-edged sword. Feedback is great and it continues be an important part of advancing our learning. However, it's a fine line between how we interpret feedback and who is providing it. Feedback can be very dangerous if it's used by others who are not experts or in a position to provide it. Be mindful of how you interpret feedback and who is giving it to you.

My son had done very well in school in grade four. He won the public speaking contest for his grade. He made hundreds in his spelling tests. And yet, his teacher gave him a C for English. I recalled that when I was in grade four, I had won the public speaking contest and received high marks and even four whole dollars and a certificate. And so I realized I could not change this teacher and the year was up, but that I could, in this instance, show my son that some people's feedback won't mean anything to you in life. I bid on a package at a tourism event and got a sweet deal and drove my son to the Whistler Ski Resort for the weekend in a Maserati sports car. We blared rock tunes on the radio the whole way and had long talks about the measure being the results. He had achieved the results in my eyes and I was very proud of him and ensured that he got the right feedback and the right message. I spent no energy on discrediting this teacher–I moved on. The year was almost up and I am my son's first teacher, so he knows where the feedback that matters lies. It would have been nice had the teacher acknowledged my son's talents in public speaking and English. But since she could not, my son learned a very valuable philosophical lesson. His sense of worth and ability to recognize his own gifts does not lie with others, regardless of their position of authority. That's key. It lies within himself and the friends and family who support him.

What are your talents?

So now that you've said it: "work to your talents," three times. What are your talents? And I don't mean just what you're paid to do, or what you have to do. What are your talents–the gifts you were given that are unique to you?

What are the things that charge you up and excite you? What are the things you do that make others respond to you in positive ways?

These are *your* talents.

To uncover your talents is as easy as tapping into what you're truly grateful for. The simplest and quickest way to get to a full list of your talents and skills is to take a page from the philosophy classic, *The Meditations*, by Marcus Aurelius.

Create your own leadership meditations. When Marcus Aurelius wrote the *The Meditations*, he was considered one of the greatest leaders on earth. He ruled during incredible strife and upheaval in Rome. Many presidents and leaders have *The Meditations*, on their bedside table. I often get excited and e-mail quotes from *The Meditations*, written back in 170 AD! I am sure my friends and colleagues cringe when they receive quotes filled with "thous" and "wilts" and "shalls" of ancient writing, so I will spare you the 170 AD writing style and use my own meditations as a real-life example of the exercise that you can use to create your own meditations.

When you complete your own "meditations" you will have a strong sense of what your talents and skills are. This is the first step to clarity and the path to leadership. In the opening of *The Meditations*, Marcus Aurelius wrote about whom he had learned from and what he was grateful for. Because of this conscious exercise, he was able to focus upon his strengths and talents.

By creating your own "meditations," you will be able to see with clarity what is good in your life, what strengths and talents you can be grateful for and, later on, you will be able to see where there are gaps. Read on, enjoy, and get inspired. At the end of my personal meditations, there is an exercise on filling in the gaps in your own "meditations." Remember, only *your* meditations will work for you. It takes reflection and some quiet time to establish them. Quiet time can be found anywhere, from a good run or walk—the best time to get answers, to taking a shower, doing the dishes or during your daily drive or bus ride home. It is usually when the world stops by accident that we get to reflect and get in touch with our thoughts. Focusing hard on reflection may not necessarily provide the meditations you are seeking. In our modern world, we often need to maximize our time.

If you do have the time to spare, curl up in a cozy chair with no interruptions and reflect every day. You deserve it.

When you begin to write down your own personalized "meditations," think about the person, challenge or opportunity that has influenced you and given you your own unique gifts. To make this even clearer, I have written down my own personal "meditations" to provide you with an idea of how to create your own. By doing these exercises you will begin to see how even the most negative experiences have been great teachers and that some good has come out of it to form your skills.

While on campaign between 170 A.D. and 180 A.D., Aurelius wrote his "meditations" as a source for his own guidance and self-improvement.

My Meditations

From my mother: I learned that I could be and do anything I wanted.

From my father: I learned the importance of music and how each of us must find our own connection with music. At the age of 60, he took up the piano and now plays the organ for his church choir.

From my sister: I learned the importance of living the big picture on the smallest of levels—to practice what I preach at all times and on every level. She taught me to embrace and protect the environment and to question the mainstream media. She showed me that it's more than all right to be alternative in taste.

From my children: I have learned the most valuable lesson of bringing play into our home lives. I have learned to balance discipline and play to a level that my children consider to be superhuman "teacher" abilities.

From my public school teachers: I continue to admire how many of them chose to forgo a higher paid career in the university track because they saw the importance of building our foundations in the public school system. Their delight in my accomplishments and high expectations of me are what lit the fire in my ambitions and fed us intellectually when we had little resources at home.

From my first mentor in university: I learned to work towards keeping my ego even and centred—not to let people's high opinions of me inflate my ego, nor to let people's low opinions of me lower my sense of who I am. He taught me to stay firm and in balance with a strong sense of self.

From my older mentors: I am grateful that they live on in me, and that I continue to carry their good messages. I am in awe that they saw who I am today all those years ago. In the face of over-confident youth, they were patient and invested time in talking, sharing their wisdom, and shaping me. And I am most grateful for the rare opportunities to mirror back their wisdom, as if it was stored inside of me to be returned to them in their own times of need.

From past judgmental bosses: I am grateful for their complete undervaluing of my skills and talents, for as the sophists believe, you learn as much from the people you don't admire as you do from those you do admire. I am grateful for having found the courage to walk away from bosses who walked with puffed-out chests and judgment, to launch my own dream—my company. For had they not been so smug, I would still be back in my cubicle, working for them. For their inability to lead, I thank them for launching my gift of leadership.

From the women's movement: I learned a most important thing—that it is not enough to want to create equal representation in government. I learned that the only way to create equal representation is to have smart women and smart men working together. A group of all women seeking equal partnership with men is a contradiction. I discovered the very real need for a cultural shift in thinking by women.

From my Rotary Club: I learned the importance of having older, wiser people in my life. They have shown us the importance of having a family in Rotary. I am so in awe of their capacity to help the community and the support each individual demonstrates within the Club. I learned to ask myself the four truths—is it the truth, is it fair to all, will it create goodwill and friendship, and will it be beneficial to all every day of my life and in all that I do?

From fear and worry: I learned they offer nothing in return. There is absolutely nothing worth worrying about or being afraid of. When people demonstrate fear, I learned to step away from it to ensure that it does not affect me. The amazing thing is that success flourishes in the absence of fear. When you walk through your fears and act with courage, you will always be rewarded. Perhaps not immediately—but ultimately you will be rewarded, and you will be able to trace all rewards back to your courageous acts. It is most important that if your work environment becomes a place of fear, you must find ways to temporarily remove yourself from it or it will begin to affect you as negatively as those around you.

From those who gossip: I learned they are at a base level of being human—for if they were enlightened and living their highest and truest self, they would be too busy living and would spend less time commenting on others.

From those who challenge me with skewed perspectives: I learned to be comfortable in speaking the truth, even if people are not happy with what I say. I have learned to try and refrain from talking of truths that will hurt. However, when challenged or called upon, I will always speak my mind.

From spending my childhood below the poverty level: I have been given the gift of a strong work ethic and an appreciation for the smallest things. I am grateful that we had little growing up; I expect no monetary things from anyone and am always pleased when the results of my work ethic allow me to enjoy the pleasures and rewards of my hard work.

From the kindness of the rural neighbours who helped raised my sister and me: I learned the importance of smiling at my neighbours and looking out for the people around me.

From the kindness of Maggie Moore and her daughter, Rebecca: I was shown a second family when I needed it most. For they exposed me to theatre, music, manners and unconditional friendship. They were patient with me as I learned to walk in their world and always accepted me for who I am. Two decades later, I learned that the trust they showed me is as important now as it was then. Rebecca's reviewing of this book, as I wrote, it encouraged me on days when I really needed to be cheered on.

From being born with a hearing impairment: I have been given the greatest gift. I have learned that a handicap is a blessing if you choose to see it. My hearing impairment has trained me to read people's body language and to see in their eyes what is true and what they are really saying. It has also taught me to look into people's eyes and to listen to them. This allows me to let people know they matter by not taking my eyes off their faces during conversations in order to look at the latest person that has entered the room. One of the most important things you can do for anyone is to let them know that what they're saying is important—70 per cent of our communication is through body language. Looking at someone when they speak, looking into their eyes, allows me to hear them in enlightened ways that the ears are not capable of.

From great politicians: I learned that for us to move men, women, boys and girls forward socially, we must have more smart women working with smart men. Therefore, it is our responsibility to do what we can to get the right people in government on all levels. The first step is to observe women candidates—learn more about them, and if they support our vision for community, we must get out and vote for them. If they move us at a higher level, we should volunteer. And if they inspire us to lead, then we must consider running for government ourselves.

From the less than ethical politicians: I learned that it is paramount for smart women and men to walk through their fear of daunting organizations and run for office. Nothing should keep great people from office. Recognize that leadership is all about service—it's not about the candidate, but the people the candidate will serve. As in Rotary, true leaders serve and the leadership grows out of their service.

From being born female: I learned that as great as the challenges are in a patriarchal society, cultural change begins with one person and moves to the many. I learned that the gifts of intuition and "gut instinct" designed to protect our young can be translated into many skills in the professional world, and for that I am grateful.

As you will see in the "meditations" I wrote above, there are gifts in the challenges of life for you to sift out. It's easy to see the gifts from the good; it's a bit more challenging and far more rewarding to find the gifts in the not so good—the hardships of life. This is where you really begin to see your strengths.

To quote Marcus Aurelius, "You will never be given more burden in life than you can bear." We will never be given more hardship than we can handle. That is a powerful realization. When we begin to understand this, we can start to seek out the meaning in hardship rather than adopt a "why me" attitude? So it is vital that we understand in every challenge or hardship, there is a nugget of gold that we can sift out from the murkiness of hardship during our lives.

To recap my own personal "meditations," my greatest gifts were being born poor and hearing impaired. The gift of poverty gave me my work ethic and enthusiastic gratitude for the smallest things and the necessary ability to practice moderation. The gift of my hearing impairment forced me to look into the eyes of every person I meet and to focus on listening so that I can hear them. This allows me to see what is really being said.

When I was in University studying journalism, I was chosen by my radio documentary professor to do a commentary for CBC Radio in Halifax. I wrote a commentary on love, and it aired on Valentine's Day. I was very excited to do this, especially for my radio professor, Dick Miller, one of the greatest radio documentary makers in Canada.

As we left the studio, I was explaining that sometimes it was hard for me to hear him in the studio because his moustache prevented me from reading his lips. Upon learning of my hearing challenges, he mentioned that I did slur some of my words ever so slightly, and he picked up on it because he was a professional producer of human sounds. I was so excited to learn this. It made perfect sense. If I could not hear very clearly, then how could I learn to communicate clearly? And somehow, I was the one who aired not only in Halifax, but due to popular request, across Canada. Not bad for a hearing impaired woman with a slight slur!

And so I began to "rain in Spain" myself by focusing harder than ever on how I pronounced my words. This grew to serve me well, and by working on this challenge, I have been able to gain the confidence and skill to give speeches, emcee large events and do interviews on CBC Radio and Television with confidence and clarity.

So the gifts and talents show up in both the good and the sometimes not so good. If I became focused on seeing these things as "obstacles," then they would have been just that—obstacles. Instead, I chipped away at the challenges and burrowed down to discover my own truth. Who says you can't go to university without money or parents to drive you there? I took out loans and jumped on the bus. My roommate gave me sheets for my bed and life began to soar.

Drafting your own personal "meditations" will allow you to discover timeless philosophies that will strengthen you personally and professionally as you carry the goodness into your everyday life and work.

Marcus Aurelius wrote nearly 2,000 years ago, and yet the messages stand the test of time. It really shows us that no matter what century or decade, people are by nature the same. We can learn from the philosophies of the past to create a profound modern day life for ourselves.

Making a resolution to create your own personal "meditations" requires a commitment to take time and reflect. Taking time to reflect is absolutely essential to forging a path of leadership. Life is all about the lessons. The process of drafting your own "meditations" will allow you to reflect upon what you have learned so far.

Take some time now to draft your personal meditations

On being playful

In my work I am very playful. I like to come up with cheeky, fun marketing campaigns for my clients. Being a Maritimer, I have, by default, a self-deprecating sense of humour and often laugh at the ridiculousness of life. It makes work fun, even when it feels stressful.

A friend once observed that I was playful at work, but not at home. I didn't pay much attention to this, as I believed my job was to discipline and socialize my children so that they would have every opportunity I didn't have as a young child. It wasn't until I brought my son to work one day to drop off a gift for a client that it became very clear that I needed to incorporate play into my home life.

We were visiting a business friend, and a couple of us had gone in on a gift certificate for golf shoes to thank her for one of the countless favours she had done for us. My son and I entered the back administrative room where her offices were. His first comment was, "Are you sure we're allowed to go in here?" I smiled and said, "Yes."

When we got up to the reception desk, the happy lady who had gotten to know me smiled and said, "Who's this young man?" I told her with pride that this was my son Victor and we were heading out to spend the day together. Her face beamed and she said, "Aren't you a lucky boy to have such a fun mommy!!" Victor kind of looked confused and wondered who she was talking about. I then realized with clarity that one of my gifts was my joy and playfulness at work, but I had not brought it into the home.

I made a commitment that day to be more playful with my children, to make them laugh, to laugh at their jokes, to be silly and share in the irony of life with them. For me, the moment that proved I had been successful in incorporating my playfulness into our personal lives happened one day when my children and I were shopping over the Christmas Holidays. My son looked at me and paid me the highest compliment. He said, "You know what mom, you would make a great teacher." I was taken aback, since I believe that teachers have the most important job on this earth. I asked him why he said that and he told me it was because I had the right amount of strictness and the right amount of fun. I am my child's first teacher.

Debbie's Story

I have the good fortune to walk in the company of human beings who live with greatness. And then, every so often when the world challenges them, they show a side of themselves that is so majestic and dignified I am completely humbled to have ever been in their company. It's as if they are transformed through hardship into these giant-sized angels.

My friend Debbie is one of these unique human beings who, through her quiet determination to build a better world in the face of the most unimaginable challenges, gives us all the courage to find wisdom from within.

Debbie is the fiancée of my good friend, Captain Trevor Greene.

Here are some questions I asked Debbie so that you may see first-hand the way an ordinary woman reveals her extraordinary wisdom

How has Trevor's philosophy of courage and justice in his work to protect others influenced you and how you lead?

Debbie: Trevor has an unspoken moral virtue in his dogma of behaviour. He treats everyone with respect, right down to the downtrodden in the downtown eastside of Vancouver or the homeless men of Japan. He leads by example. Trevor used to say to me that he would never ask his men to do something he wasn't willing to do. He also told me how the officers of a platoon lead from the front of the line. This shows how important it is to lead by example. To lead by example, you have to have courage, since you may be the first to face the enemy.

Trevor had a very serious injury occur in Afghanistan and you continue to support his work and belief in serving the people there and protecting women and children. How did you come to this big picture thinking?

Debbie: When I realized I might never again see the greatest love of my life, I reflected on what he is like as a person. Trevor's character embraces the philosophical principles of the likes of Marcus Aurelius. He lives life like he is on a mission to make this world a better place. What attracted me most to him is his passion for life and his mindful, ethical actions. He is extremely zealous about absolutely everything he engages in and anyone he engages with. Trevor puts his whole heart and soul into everything he does. His life is about making a difference. He put his life on the line to help others in another country fraught with instability. What was I doing? I was building my career as a young chartered accountant. I was planning to make a name for myself in the business world. When the attack happened, it made me realize how brief our time is on earth and how I was spending my time. Was I making the world a better place for my daughter for other people's daughters? No. Was I going to be proud of my accomplishments for this planet? No.

I always believed in Trevor and the Canadian mission in Afghanistan, but it took this assault on Trevor for me to really "get it." By getting it, I mean the bigger picture—the bigger question about our purpose here on earth. I started to question my ambitions in life and Trevor's ambitions. They were not congruent. I was worried about losing the greatest love of my life and what I would do if I could erase the attack on him. I would live every moment with him like it was our last and ensure his mission is not left undone.

What would you want other women to learn from this experience of yours and from Trevor?

Debbie:

- Life is a learning experience. The present is only the present, it is not the future.

- Have courage. Show faith. Be patient. Trust God. Approach everything with aplomb.

- Show love like you've never shown it before.

- Don't stress about what might never be.

- If given the right conditions, the mind can be the greatest tool in the healing process.

- Put yourself first. You can't help anyone if you don't help yourself first.

- Stay within your limits to stay sane.

- Ask for help; accept help from family and friends.

- Take solace from family and friends.

- It is so important that a loved one in the hospital environment has an advocate to speak for him or her.

- Question absolutely everything the health care team is doing for your loved one.

Wonder is the beginning of wisdom.

– GREEK PROVERB

VII

Beauty

VII

Dulce est desipere in loco. Woe to philosophers who cannot laugh away their wrinkles. I look upon solemnity as a disease.

– VOLTAIRE

The sculpture is already there in the raw stone; the task of a good sculptor is merely to eliminate the unnecessary parts of the stone.

– MICHELANGELO

This philosophical belief by the famed artist, Michelangelo, is really how we, as women, must view our own bodies as beautiful as in art. And if art is interpretive, then each of us has our own unique physical beauty that truly comes from within. So how do we uncover our beauty and reveal our own unique "art" to the world? We start with the Taoist quote, "Return to the uncarved block."

I met a young girl at a friend's birthday party. She was bright beyond her years and had written beautiful stories and poems to help a dear friend who was in the hospital. When her mother mentioned that the little girl was worried about her weight, I, like many women, could relate. And the one thing that really resonated for this little girl was the analogy of her beauty being her gift of writing, her deep thoughtfulness and sparkle, and any excess weight is merely clay—the clay that falls away from the beautiful sculpture within. I asked her if she would spend any amount of energy focusing on the stuff that gets tossed away when an artist is making a sculpture. She said no. So together, we came to the conclusion that her energies would be better spent by just focusing upon the sculpture, her work, her thoughtfulness, her joy, and allowing the sculpture to present itself rather than putting all that energy into stuff that does not matter.

Your *expression* is your beauty–this should be valued far above form

I find Michelangelo fascinating. The fact that this genius of an artist believed that the art work was already hidden in the clay and that our task is to uncover the work of art within, can be applied to everything from our own bodies to the city.

When I lost my weight in my youth, I always visualized a strong, beautiful work of art hidden beneath the extra pounds, waiting to be uncovered. The same can be applied to anyone who is struggling with weight: your true, healthful, work of art is already inside, and once you have struck that mind-body-spirit harmony, your work of art will reveal itself.

For the city, when facing urban decay I see the same work of art waiting within. When we visualize what a commercial area can look like, cleaned up and with a bustling vibrant merchants' area that merges the arts, commerce and residents to create a sense of place, we are visualizing a work of art waiting to be uncovered. And this work of art will only emerge when the city is governed by all three levels of the tripartite soul working in harmony. Recall the model of economic development that followed Jean-Jacques Rousseau's Social Contract, whereby everyone has a seat at the table to ensure that, regardless of gender or socio-economic status, everyone is working together to uncover the work of art hidden beneath the decay.

Michelangelo

It has been said that Michelangelo's gift was his ability to see beauty and grandness everywhere, even though no one else could see it. He was said to be divinely gifted in his ability to see this beauty and that he had the practical ability to convert what he saw into a reality for others through his sculptures and paintings.

Michelangelo felt that we must NOT place form over expression, since it is far easier to copy beauty and other people's idea of beauty as reflected in popular trends, than to discover your own beauty from inside yourself. For that is the true beauty he felt was most authentic, and in the end, most sought after. Michelangelo's art was built upon two key concepts: dignity and power which supersede any trendy notion of beauty.

Beauty and the idea of beauty have changed throughout the centuries. If you look at past eras you can see that being voluptuous was the trend of beauty for the day and in other times, like the era of Twiggy, it was the skinny woman who was considered beautiful. Michelangelo believed we must get past the temporary trend of beauty of the day and get back to authentic internal beauty which is founded on your own dignity and your own power. He felt that when the form of the beauty was placed over the expression from within, you were left with "inferior excellence."

This is a very, very important point. For this divine concept of beauty extends to us as women. When your beauty comes from within, from that place of who you are—a place of dignity and knowledge of your own power as a human being to pursue right action—you will be far more beautiful than any magazine cover.

Michelangelo created masterpieces with the characteristics of majesty and grandeur. His art showcased character and moral force.

Think about that—character and moral force are to be the first consideration, your top priority. Your expression is your beauty—far above the form of your body.

Think of yourself as a work of art

I believe that words used to describe great expressive art should be used instead for women's beauty. Instead of the words, pretty, cute, or even beautiful, we should try to use the words that Michelangelo used to describe a work of art.

So to shift our thinking, try these words to describe yourself, your daughters, or female friends and colleagues when explaining how they look and behave. Your focus should be on their expression, not their form.

Bold   Majestic   Dignified   Original

Creative   Expressive   Visionary

Strong   Handsome/Beautiful   Head High

Chin Up   Noble Purpose

Exuberant   Philosophically Directed   Powerful

All my life, I've battled weight. When I was 15 years old, I had reached 210 pounds and could not walk past a school bus without being called names by the other children. Just prior to going into high school, I had a "turning point" moment that forever changed the way I view weight and how to get a handle on it. Not only was it unhealthy, it was undermining my confidence in my other talents—my weight was simply getting in the way of all the living I was put on this earth to do.

One night at a birthday party I sat down with a close friend and commented on how amazing her sister looked who had recently lost 60 lbs. I was so in awe and said, "I wish I could do that." My friend looked at me and answered, "Sure you can, and you know what? You will be so beautiful, because I can see that your face will be beautiful when it's better defined."

And that was it. I realized then, from her words, that my face and body were like a sculpture hidden away inside the clay of the excess weight and my job was to do the work to allow my beautiful inner sculpture to come forth. And that's what I did.

I lost 60 pounds and when I walked into my new high school—no one recognized me! A few boys did come up and admit to me that they always said I'd be beautiful if I lost weight, but no one told me. I only recalled being called names by the other children when I was overweight. I was also intrigued by the strangers, the folks whom I didn't know but who knew of me and what I had done. Some of them would come up and introduce themselves and tell me how in awe they were of what I had accomplished, but that they were intimidated by me and didn't know how to approach me and talk about it. So it started to dawn on me that this new state of physical beauty brought with it an inner strength that could not be seen or felt by others or myself until the excess, unnecessary parts of me were removed.

Years later when I had both of my children, I gained a lot of weight. But each time I lost the weight by living the virtue of moderation. If you follow the virtues, they will enable you to stay on your proper track.

So there should really be no discussion of what I ate, or how much I ate, or how much I exercised. The point isn't to follow *my* path—you need to stay true to what fits *your* sense of moderation. It's your sculpture—no one can tell you how to reveal your inner beauty.

And no one can or has the right to tell you what your ideal of beauty is—you already know that. You know your body better than anyone and what your strong points are and what you need to work on.

Return to the un-carved block

So instead of providing a diet plan of how to eat and when to eat and when to exercise, here is the philosophical guide to uncovering the sculpture within.

The ancient philosophers looked at beauty as art. Therefore, if we cast off the current societal pressures of beauty and begin to see ourselves as art, then we're seeing ourselves though a different lens, one that is less stressful and far more enjoyable. We will see this as more of a creative process rather than a diet.

Mind, body and spirit connection

We applaud ourselves as a society for being smart (mind) and we applaud ourselves for being philanthropic and donating to worthy causes or through volunteerism (spirit) but who applauds you when you go for a run at lunch (body)?

Our society is rapt with the notion of the mind, body, and spirit connection. But somewhere we've forgotten about the body in a healthy, balanced way. Or worse yet, we obsess about it, which is the other extreme, and in the obsessing lose all perspective on how to get on with it and just get the workouts done.

Remember, this is a guide to discovering what works best for your life to ensure you are doing all the things you need to lead and live the best life intended for you and the people who have been brought into your life.

Time Tested Beauty Tips

For attractive lips, speak words of kindness.

For lovely eyes, seek out the good in people.

For a slim figure, share your food with the hungry.

For beautiful hair, let a child run his fingers through it once a day.

For poise, walk with the knowledge you'll never walk alone...

People, even more than things, have to be restored, renewed, revived, reclaimed, and redeemed and redeemed and redeemed. Never throw out anybody.

Remember, if you ever need a helping hand, you'll find one at the end of your arm. As you grow older, you will discover that you have two hands. One for helping yourself, the other for helping others.

– SAM LEVENSON

The famous actress and Unicef ambassador, Audrey Hepburn, lived by this poem and made it famous by her reference to it. It was the last thing she read to her family before she passed on.

Beauty defined as harmony

Throughout the ages, beauty has been defined as harmony. If we are in harmony with our mind, body and spirit, we become the highest level of beauty.

Exuberance is beauty

– WILLIAM BLAKE

We all know women who have the physical proportions of beauty, but may not demonstrate the spirit of beauty or kindness and for that there seems to be something missing, almost as if there is a dullness to the form of their beauty. We also know women who may not have the proportion of a beauty, but their spirit lights up the room and people flock to them. Exuberance *is* Beauty.

We know, as Marcus Aurelius stated, that beauty comes from within. Would it not stand to reason that a balanced, well-proportioned life is the definition of beauty? So then, why would you waste your energies chasing down another's idea of beauty when you already know what it takes to lead a well balanced, proportioned life for yourself more than any one else can tell you.

> *Anything in any way beautiful derives its beauty from itself, and asks nothing beyond itself. Praise is no part of it, for nothing is made worse or better by praise. This applies even to the more mundane forms of beauty: natural objects, for example, or works of art. What need has true beauty of anything further? Surely none; any more than law, truth, or kindness or modesty. Is any of these embellished by praise, or spoiled by censure? Does the emerald lose its beauty by lack of admiration? Does gold, or ivory, or purple? A lyre or a dagger, a rosebud or a sapling?*

– MARCUS AURELIUS

I particularly relate to this quote by Marcus Aurelius. For if you think of it, is an emerald beautiful because someone says it is? Or is it simply beautiful on its own? Aren't we beautiful in unusual ways regardless of the beauty norms our culture dictates? I put this into practice. As women, we often scrutinize our breasts. And for those of us who have had children, often they just don't look the same as they did before. I know I went from a full B to less than an A! There was a time when I was considering having implants. Many of my friends had had this done and were so happy with the results. I continued to grapple with this idea of beauty and wondered for myself, whose idea of beauty is that?

I have been so supportive of my friends' decisions and wondered if this would work me. Until one day, I saw myself in my true beauty. I had an old dress on and was cleaning the bathrooms. And again, doing manual work allows your subconscious mind to give you the answers to the challenges you have proposed. There I was with cleanser all over me, my hair was a mess and I caught a glimpse of myself in the mirror. Oddly, I noticed how my chest closely resembled that of a ballerina. The ability to vaguely see the ribs on my barrel chest looked so much like a dancer's chest. That night when I was getting ready to go to an event, I decided that with such small breasts, I could wear a gorgeous black dress with a plunging neckline to show off my ballerina chest. This is something I had never done before. And that night, I was surprised at how many compliments I received on my dress and was surprised by the large-breasted women who came up to me and said, "I wish I could wear a dress like yours." So in the end, it dawned on me. If I believe I am beautiful, and I see the beauty in its honesty and embrace it for what it is—so will everyone else. The power resides in me.

This is important in everything you do. If you see what the value is in something and you believe it, so will everyone else around you. Therefore, it is important to connect with what is authentic for you in your beauty—not what the ideal is for everyone around you. I do not wish to deter my friends from making their decisions about their beauty. It is crucial that we not judge each other, but rather work toward becoming our most authentic selves.

The most beautiful model in the world is a role model.

REFERENCES

Addison, Paul. *Churchill–The Unexpected Hero.* Oxford; Oxford University Press, 2005

Cranston, Maurice. *Jean-Jacques Rousseau–The Social Contract.* London; Penguin Classics, 2004

Davies, Smith. *Women who Changed the World.* London; Smith Davies, 2006

Frankl, Viktor. *Man's Search for Meaning.* Boston; Beacon Press, 2006

Gilbert, Martin. *Churchill and the Jews.* Ontario; McClelland & Stewart Ltd., 2007

Hammond, Martin. *Marcus Aurelius–The Meditations.* London; Penguin Classics, 2006

Lavine, T.Z. *From Socrates to Sartre; the Philosophic Quest.* London; Bantam Books, 1989

Lebell, Sharon. *Epictetus–The Art of Living.* New York; Harper-Collins, 1994

Maltz, Maxwell. *The New Psycho Cybernetics.* New Jersey, Prentice Hall Press, 2003

O'Donnell, Kevin. *A History of Ideas.* Oxford; Lion Publishing, 2003

Stokes, Philip. *Philosophy–100 Essential Thinkers.* Ontario; Indigo Books, 2006

Wicks, Ben. *Born to Read.* Toronto; Ben Wicks & Associates, 1995

Wollstonecraft, Mary. *A Vindication of the Rights of Women.* London; Penguin Books, 2004

Interviews

Personal interview with Diane Thorne, MLA, Coquitlam-Maillardville, Coquitlam, British Columbia, Canada, Jan. 2007.

Personal interview with Irene Barr, Former President of the Women's Commission for a Provincial political party in BC, Port Coquitlam, British Columbia, Canada, Feb. 2007.

Personal interview with Nasima Nastoh, Motivational Speaker for the rights of youth, Coquitlam, British Columbia, Canada, Feb. 2007.

Personal interview with Jovilyn Mercy Culasing, Nanny, Port Moody, British Columbia, Canada, Jan. 2007.

Personal interview with Lisa Palleson-Stallan, Owner Lotuswear, West Vancouver, British Columbia, Jan. 2007.

Personal interview with Debbie Lepore, fiancée of Captain Trevor Greene, Kitsilano, British Columbia, Feb. 2007.

Personal interview with Dr. Colin Starnes, Former President of the University of King's College, Halifax, Nova Scotia, May 2006.

Reports

Elizabeth Haggart and Kristel vom Scheidt (2005) Final Report of the Women in Local Government Project—*Untapped Resources—Women in Municipal Government in Nova Scotia*. Halifax, Nova Scotia. Oct. 2005

ABOUT THE AUTHOR

Journalist, Business Professional and Motivational Speaker, Barb Stegemann, takes philosophy out of the university classrooms. With the help of ordinary women doing extraordinary things, she shows how ancient philosophy can be used every day in the real world of modern women.

Barb Stegemann is a real-life example of the power of philosophy and self-discovery in leading a happy and successful life. She came from humble beginnings and, through the power of philosophy and visualization, uncovered, and continues to discover the leader within. Guided by a vision that she could make a difference, nothing has prevented her from reaching her goals. She founded Acclimatize Communications Corp., a company that has helped large corporations and government organizations adapt to their changing environments. She gives talks to women and business professionals on economic development, and delivers talks to youth on visualization. She's made it her life's work to empower people to tap into the answers they already have.

Her work has been featured in *BC Business* and *The Block* magazines. She is called upon for interviews as an expert on the issues she discusses in this book by *The Globe & Mail, Business in Vancouver, Atlantic Business Magazine, CBC TV, CBC Radio, Radio Canada, CKNW Radio, City TV, the Andrew Krystal Show, the Rick Howe Show* and other media. She writes a column called "Culture Shift" for The Chronicle Herald's business section. Her focus on economic development for Nova Scotia through her column is helping to change the way the economy is viewed by her community.

Barb believes that building women's networks with smart men and women is the most important route to advancing women in politics and business, and ultimately narrowing the gap between rich and poor. Her talks and company have tipped a new movement of empowering women to gain influence within predominantly male networks. She has recognized and brought to the forefront of our consciousness the idea that until women as individuals network with women *and* men, we will continue to have children living in poverty. Barb Stegemann has brought into reality her vision for a women-centred leadership model based on the same principles of classical philosophy that men have used for centuries. And thus *The 7 Virtues of a Philosopher Queen* was born.

Visit The 7 Virtues Web site for details on how to host a speaking engagement/fundraiser that will advance your organization with Barb Stegemann.

www.the7virtues.com